Contents

February

March

April

May

Summer Holidays: 3rd Sunday in May to Early August

PRAYERS, PAPERS, & PLAY

Devotions for Every College Student

Barbara Canale

Liguori

Imprimi Potest:
Harry Grile, CSsR, Provincial
Denver Province, The Redemptorists

Published by Liguori Publications
Liguori, Missouri 63057

To order, call 800-325-9521
Liguori.org

Copyright © 2013 Barbara Canale

All rights reserved. No part of this publication may be reproduced, stored in a retrieval system, or transmitted in any form or by any means—electronic, mechanical, photocopy, recording, or any other—except for brief quotations in printed reviews, without the prior written permission of Liguori Publications.

Library of Congress Cataloging-in-Publication Data
Canale, Barbara S.
  Prayers, papers, and play : devotions for every college student / Barbara S. Canale. – 1st ed.
     p. cm.
  1. College students–Prayers and devotions. 2. Catholic Church–Prayers and devotions.
  I. Title.
  BX2373.S8C35 2013
  242'.634–dc23
                                        2012042162
p ISBN: 978-0-7648-2154-7

e ISBN: 978-0-7648-6809-2

Excerpts from English translation of the Catechism of the Catholic Church for the United States of America © 1994, United States Catholic Conference, Inc.— *Libreria Editrice Vaticana*; English translation of the Catechism of the Catholic Church: Modifications from the *Editio Typica* © 1997, United States Catholic Conference, Inc.—*Libreria Editrice Vaticana.*

Scripture texts in this work are taken from the *New American Bible*, revised edition © 2010, 1991, 1986, 1970 Confraternity of Christian Doctrine, Washington, D.C., and are used by permission of the copyright owner. All Rights Reserved. No part of the *New American Bible* may be reproduced in any form without permission in writing from the copyright owner.

Compliant with *The Roman Missal*, third edition.

Liguori Publications, a nonprofit corporation, is an apostolate of The Redemptorists. To learn more about The Redemptorists, visit Redemptorists.com.

Cover Design: John Krus
Cover Images: Shutterstock

Printed in the United States of America
22 21 20 19 18 / 6 5 4 3 2
First Edition

Dedication

This book is dedicated to Juliana and Andrea Canale

Acknowledgments

To Patrick, I extend my heartfelt gratitude for his willingness to support me through this endeavor. I thank him for listening, for his brilliant ideas, insight, and input.

I thank my selfless parents, Joseph and Barbara Casper, who gave me my faith, fostering it throughout my life, with an infinite stream of love and encouragement.

This book wouldn't be complete without acknowledging my friend and pastor, Reverend Monsignor J. Robert Yeazel, for his friendship, his spiritual guidance, and immeasurable words of inspiration.

I am sincerely grateful to Christy Hicks of Liguori Publications, who believed in this project and worked tirelessly with the patience of a saint to see it through to completion. Thank you for making it possible to enrich the lives of college students everywhere. Our future is their hands.

To my loving Lord, who gives me everything—I thank you for it all.

Introduction

When my daughter, Juliana, attended her freshman year in college, there wasn't a chapel on campus, and the nearest church was more than a mile away. In a remote town in northern New York state, she was sometimes required to hike monstrous snowbanks to get to Mass each Sunday. She took a leap of faith and vowed to maintain her faithfulness to God. Because her campus did not host Bible studies or have a Newman Center, I e-mailed daily devotions to her. And I tried to cater them around the events on campus: the teachers she met, the classes she took and the clubs she joined. Because college is hectic, it is challenging to balance the many aspects of life on campus: spiritual, intellectual, emotional, financial, and social.

The devotions I sent her reinforced that God had a magnificent plan for my daughter, if she could just hold on and trust in the Lord. As Juliana graduates, I want to pass along some of the ideas I generated for her to help you through school, and to support you on your journey through college. *Prayers, Papers, and Play* is intended to help all college students achieve a balanced life, which is in reality a life that is whole, or holy.

The format is unique and written with your schedule in mind. This devotion begins in mid-August and ends in mid-May, with twelve summer themes to think on during your summer holidays. Furthermore, each week Fridays and Saturdays are combined, as it is likely at the end of the week that your schedule will be less structured. I wove in stories about saints that might intrigue you or pertain to an issue you might be struggling with, but the most important message of the devotional is: Pray every day. God is with you and desires to accompany you.

Also, I tried to estimate when most schools would be celebrating homecoming weekends, exams, and school breaks. If I didn't get your school to follow the devotional exactly, you can skip ahead to the weeks that pertain to your school's schedule. In the back are twelve special reflections to cover the summer weeks, but I encourage you to read them over winter break to plan ahead for summer.

Let the Lord speak to you through these pages. It is no mistake that you are holding this book today. Read this devotional every day and keep the Lord in your life. Before you know it, you will be graduating, too. Enjoy the journey!

Mid-August

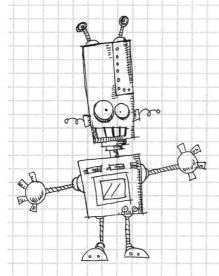

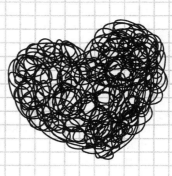

New Beginnings

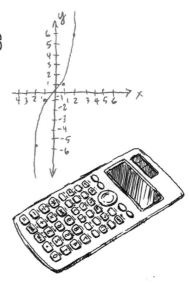

Sunday

"The LORD said to Abram: Go forth from your land, your relatives, and from your father's house to a land that I will show you" (Genesis 12:1).

Have courage by walking with God. It can be unnerving to step outside of your comfort zone as you transition into campus life. Apprehensiveness melts away when you turn to God, who will fortify you. On the feast of the Assumption of Mary, recall the difficulties and trepidations she experienced with her transitions. God watched over her just as he will safeguard you. To develop stability with God, turn to prayer. How often will you include prayer in your daily routine? God is always with you, guiding and protecting you as you begin school. As you navigate your campus this week, remember that God is walking beside you.

Dear God,

Wrap your loving arms around me as I embark on a new life in college near the feast of Mary's Assumption. Guide me on my journey and keep me safe, as you protected Mary. Allow me to absorb the experiences you have provided and teach me to embrace all that is good on this campus. I love you, Lord. Amen.

Monday

"A time to seek, and a time to lose" (Ecclesiastes 3:6).

Include God in your plans. God directed your path to your university because that is where he wants you to be. You are standing at the precipice of your collegiate journey where you will make myriad discoveries about yourself, your friends, professors, classes, and curriculum. Your time at college is precious; use it wisely. Ask God to help you to cultivate earnest study habits. This wonderful opportunity of new beginnings allows you to develop all of the positive traits and behaviors that God wants for you, to expand on them and grow. While graduation is your final destination, the worthwhile elements creating your college experience is the journey. How do you plan to make necessary changes in your life and cultivate your relationship with God at school?

> Dear God,
>
> Help me as I embark on this journey of discovering who I am and what I am made of. Make me strong and capable to withstand all that awaits me. Teach me to embrace all that is worthy and to avoid anything that could derail me. I adore you, Jesus, my Lord and Savior. Amen.

Tuesday

"Because of you my acquaintances shun me;
  you make me loathsome to them" (Psalm 88:9).

Make God your BFF. Your high school friends don't respond to your texts often enough. Are they as busy as you? Through social media you find pictures of them with new friends. Remember that the bond of true friends survives the test of time. God has provided you with a chance to develop new friendships through ultimate Frisbee competitions, presentations, concerts, and social events to welcome students to campus. Attend them with an open mind. Maybe you want to be involved with athletics, student government, or community service. How will you cultivate new relationships on campus? How will you foster your friendship with God? What can you do each day to reinforce your love of the Lord?

Dear God,

Bless my friends from home and all of the new friendships that I make on campus. Surround me with people who will make my transition to college life meaningful and happy. Help me to develop authentic bonds with students who will enrich my college experience, and help me to grow and become all that you want me to be. I love you, Lord. Amen.

Wednesday

"The noble plan noble deeds, and in noble deeds they persist" (Isaiah 32:8).

Put God in your plan. Devise plans to keep on track by setting goals. Prioritize lists of things you must do and things you want to do. Plan how to motivate yourself, through physical activities, school functions, prayer, or through other creative measures. Does your school host guest speakers whose talks you can attend? Would you like to participate in an honors program? How will you connect with God each day? How will you develop your spirituality on campus? Can you keep a list of ways to accomplish this while juggling your courses and social activities? You are pleasing God by making a plan to include him in your life at school. Though it requires concentration and effort to make a plan, it is worthwhile taking the first step toward achieving your goal, especially if God is at the top of that list.

Dear God,

Assist me in assessing my plans and goals. Guide me on my college journey. Thank you for putting wonderful ideas into my head and for placing supportive people in my path. With you, I can do anything. Amen.

Thursday

"From the ends of the earth I call; my heart grows faint. Raise me up, set me on a rock, for you are my refuge, a tower of strength against the foe" (Psalm 61:3–4).

Listen to God's advice. It is understandable to have feelings of homesickness. Ask God to give you the courage to leave the confines that are isolating. Also, ask God to help you make new friends and to give you the courage to take the first step forward. It will be the first of many that you will have to make on campus and throughout the rest of your life. What strategy will you use to listen to God's voice today? Turn off your phone and walk to class with God in your heart. Tell him the fears you harbor and listen for his reply. You might rejoice in the message he is trying to convey. Listen, and God will tell you what to do.

Dear God,

Remove my apprehensions and fill me with courage, for I so desire to be a successful student. Bring the right people into my life to help me to grow on this campus. Bless my actions and keep me in your good graces today and always. Amen.

Friday/Saturday

"What is desired of a person is fidelity" (Proverbs 19:22).

Kindness pleases God. People are fallible but basically good. Loyalty is a character trait you hope your friends possess. God gives you the opportunity to be loyal to him and to others each day, so return it abundantly and faithfully, but do so with kindness. Any gesture, regardless of the size, if it is done with kindness, it is done with love. Perhaps smile at someone you normally would not notice or join a student eating alone in the cafeteria. What other act of kindness could you do today? You might encounter classmates who don't share the same morals or values that you have. Can you offer a prayer for them instead of a harsh word? You cannot begin to know what fears or pains they harbor. God wants everyone to be treated kindly. How can you be more kind to your classmates?

Dear God,

Help me to treat everyone I meet with kindness, even though some may not deserve it. Help me to have compassion to ill-tempered people, for they need my care the most. Let me lead by my example of gentleness and consideration. Amen.

Transitions

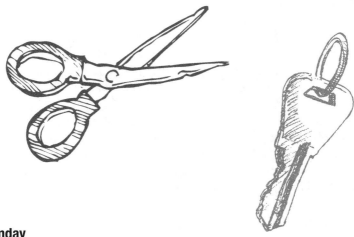

Sunday

"Be strong and steadfast! Do not fear nor be dismayed, for the LORD, your God, is with you wherever you go" (Joshua 1:9).

You are never alone. You may feel lonely because your family has returned home. Perhaps you are living in a small space and the solitude might be intimidating or frightening. But God is with you. Let God's presence settle over you and comfort you. How will you reach out to God? There will be times when you will be called upon to do something outside of your comfort zone. Maybe it is taking your first college exam, making your first presentation, or trying out for a sport. What are your concerns and how will you overcome them? Face your fears, remembering that God is beside you and the Holy Spirit dwells within you. The Lord God Almighty will not let you be harmed.

Dear God,

Remove the anxieties that surround and engulf me. Give me the determination that I need to step away from my isolation and be a successful college student. Help me, Lord, to have the courage to meet new people and establish an endearing connection with them and with you. Amen.

Monday

> "You need endurance to do the will of God and
>   receive what he has promised" (Hebrews 10:36).

Focus on God. By attending college, you are doing what
God wants. You are obtaining the skills necessary for your
life's work. Can you feel God steering you in the right
direction? Sometimes a seed of doubt gets planted when you
are busy. You may be anxious to see results, or you might
question if you are doing the right thing. Have patience,
trust, and believe that God knows what is best for you. When
you feel yourself being tested, how can you turn to God
amidst classes, obligations, and distractions? What are some
ways you can focus on God throughout this day?

Dear God,

Give me the fortitude I need to be an intelligent college
student. Open my mind to absorb the knowledge that you
are pouring over me. The courses are more challenging than
I imagined. The professors expect more than I thought they
would. Keep me focused on you, dear Lord, so that I will be
successful and please you in all that I say and do. Amen.

Tuesday

> "And his clothes became dazzling white, such as
>   no fuller on earth could bleach them" (Mark 9:3).

Ask God for humility. Perhaps you have done laundry before, but
now you are forced to share washers and dryers with your dorm mates.
Laundry is a domestic chore that few people enjoy. You must balance
emptying your trash, recycling, keeping your room orderly, and many
other boring tasks. Jesus desires you to be humble. Can you find happiness in the chores knowing they keep you grounded? Perhaps you
could offer the suffrage of the work to God. What other sacrifices can
you offer up to God? If you struggle with this, ask the Lord to give you
the patience you need to endure. When God sees that you are making
an effort, he is pleased.

Dear God,

Teach me how to multi-task the mundane chores that are expected of me. Don't let me become lethargic and let the errands pile up. Remind me to pray while I work and offer it up to you. Enlighten me so I can accomplish all of the tasks that I set out to do. Amen.

Wednesday

"(The men) are to dine with me at noon" (Genesis 43:16).

Get nourishment from God. Perhaps when you were living at home, meals were consistent or at least tasted great. Sharing a meal with family members offered a sense of hominess and stability. On campus, students face innumerable issues to locate a dining hall, select something healthy, stay on schedule, and re-energize. What options do you have to get spiritual nourishment? How do you plan to invigorate your soul on campus? In order to keep your body and soul working harmoniously, what challenges would you have to overcome to accomplish this? Is it *apropos* for you to say grace before your meals? Do you have the courage to pray when others do not? Ask God for guidance. He will steer you in the right direction.

Dear God,

Nourish my body and my soul so I can become all that I am capable of. Help me to be grateful for the food that I will eat today. There are starving people throughout the world who have nothing and yet I have so much. Bless them and the people whose stomachs growl for your spiritual nourishment. Amen.

Thursday

"Beloved, I hope you are prospering in every respect and are in good health, just as your soul is prospering" (3 John 1:2).

Safeguard your soul. It seems as if the moment one student gets sick, germs spread like wildfire and the entire campus catches it. Germs are everywhere, and sickness is inevitable. While it is important to wash your hands frequently, eat nutritious food, get plenty of rest, and exercise, it is also essential to pray. If you take precautions to prevent illness, what can you do to keep your soul resilient? Throughout the course of the day, when can you pray and spend time in spiritual reflection to keep your soul healthy? Some students pray to stay well! Include prayer in your daily regimen. What good is it if your body is strong and healthy but your soul is not? Prayer is the answer to everything.

Dear God,

Thank you for the life that you gave to me and for keeping me well. Please continue to keep me well as I delve into this semester. Watch over me while I am away from home, and bless my family. Keep me safe in your love and mercy. Amen.

Friday/Saturday

"LORD, you have been our refuge through all generations" (Psalm 90:1).

Seek refuge in the Lord. When life becomes hectic, ask God to comfort you. If your mind wanders to problems that surround you, how will you give your apprehensions to God? Because worrying is a waste of time, pray instead. Prayer can bring you closer to the Lord. God knows what you carry in your heart. Saint Martha (from the first century), patron of housewives and hotelkeepers, worried that she was doing more work than her sister, Mary, who merely sat at Jesus' feet and listened to him. Jesus told Martha to stop worrying and resign her anxiousness. Are you more like Mary or Martha?

Dear God,

I leave my problems at your feet. Take them from me and give me rest. Instill in me a greater appreciation for everything that you give to me, whether or not I like it or want it. Some day I will understand your plan and reason for everything. Teach me to stop worrying and wasting the precious time that you have given me. I know you are always with me to guide, love, and protect me on my college path. Amen.

September

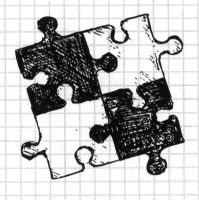

Establishing Routines

Sunday

"What profit have we from all the toil,
which we toil at under the sun?" (Ecclesiastes 1:3)

Believe, accept, and trust in God. Do you stay up late at night reading and doing assignments or projects by forgoing watching a movie, attending shows, or football games? At the end of the day, do you question what you have accomplished? You might think, why bother? You cannot see the knowledge you are gaining. You have to trust that it is there. You cannot see the skills you are acquiring; you just have to believe that you are learning. You might not be able to feel the progress you have made; accept that you are developing and growing. You cannot see God, but he is there ready, willing, and able to help you. How do you show God that you trust him? What can you do today to trust, accept, and believe that what you are doing is God's plan for you?

Dear God,

I feel your presence in my life. Let me trust in your plan, whatever it is. I am in your hands, Lord. Put me to work. I accept what you ask. Amen.

Monday

"Plans fail when there is no counsel, but they succeed
when advisors are many" (Proverbs 15:22).

Trust in God's plan for you. Are you bombarded with an overload of information from class schedules, clubs, and organizations? Stop for a moment and reflect on God's goodness in your life today. What talents do you possess, who have you befriended, what experiences have you had this week that are unique to your life place? God has placed special people in your life to draw you closer—professors, mentors, advisors, friends, and family members. These people communicate God's wisdom through their unique giftedness. Perhaps their counsel will empower you to listen to God's voice today in order to follow more directly God's will in your life.

Dear God,

Thank you for the gifts of advice that you have given to me through the staff at school. Thank you for the wisdom my parents used to raise me. I am fortunate that you brought so many wonderful people into my life to transform me into the person I am today. Thank you, Lord, for all of the blessings you have given to me today. Amen.

Tuesday

"I keep the LORD always before me; with him at my right hand I shall never be shaken....You will show me the path to life, abounding joy in your presence, the delights at your right hand forever" (Psalm 16:8, 11).

Follow God with confidence. With the plethora of professors at your university, there are many who will stand out and shape your mind in phenomenal ways. Let Jesus be your best teacher. When you journey through life with him, you might be traveling down a road less frequently taken. It is never easy plodding the course for others to follow. It might be intimidating leading the way, but God is with you. Do you follow God wherever he leads? What is the last thing God asked you to do that you completely surrendered yourself to? Go where God leads, even if it is an unfamiliar course. God will reward you for it.

Dear God,

Give me the courage to stand up and walk an uncharted path. Help me to focus on the job you want me to do. Take my hand and show me the way. Amen.

Wednesday

"A lamp from the LORD is human life-breath;
it searches through the inmost being"(Proverbs 20:27).

Please God with good intentions. Do you know people who go out of their way to be helpful? Maybe a professor, classmate, or advisor is particularly accommodating. Saint Elizabeth Ann Seton established the first congregation of religious sisters in the United States to serve underprivileged children. Her greatest difficulties were internal, stemming from misunderstandings and interpersonal conflicts. Yet her actions were self-sacrificing. God is as interested in your behaviors as he is with your motives. What can you do to keep your intentions pure? The Lord's light penetrates the human spirit, exposing every hidden motive. Do you have any hidden motives on your agenda? God gave you a mind and a conscience. How will you take accountability for your actions today?

Dear God,

Keep my intentions respectable and my behaviors just. Keep me on the straight and narrow path. Let me check my moral compass every day to ensure that I am on the right path. I want to be an honest and caring student, accountable for my actions, good or evil. I ask this in your name, Lord. Amen.

Thursday

"Do not return evil for evil, or insult for insult;
but, on the contrary, a blessing, because to this
you were called, that you might inherit a blessing"
(1 Peter 3:9).

Bless those who curse you. It would be nice if you liked everyone on campus. Because you are all different with varying backgrounds, morals, and values, you may not agree with how some students live. They might make cruel comments or hurtful offenses. Do not retaliate with rudeness when people insult you. Instead, could you pay them back with a blessing? It will not be easy, but that is exactly what God wants you to do. What else can you do besides asking God to change their ways? Maybe you could offer them a compliment or praise an academic achievement. Whatever you do, if it is done in love, God will bless you for it.

Dear God,

Fill my head with pleasant thoughts and make my heart rich with abundant love so that I have the self-control and insight to say something pleasant when I am insulted. Empower me with your wisdom and courage so that I pray for that person. Amen.

Friday/Saturday

"Remind them to be under the control of magistrates and authorities, to be obedient, to be open to every good enterprise. They are to slander no one, to be peaceable, considerate, exercising all graciousness toward everyone" (Titus 3:1–2).

Jesus' mission was love. It is not easy to do what professors expect. Sometimes their requests are unrealistic. Once the weekend arrives, the last thing you might want to do as a student is homework and projects, especially if they are not due right away. It is tempting to put it off and attend a football game or concert instead. If classmates complain about assignments and professors, what positive comments can you offer? What would Jesus say? He was an amicable person. God placed your professors in your path to help you. You depend on their knowledge for your education. Can you embrace this gift? Can you accept your assignments peaceably? Jesus' mission was love. Can you make that your mission too?

Dear God,

Help me to comply with the expectations of my parents and the college. Help me to find kind and comforting words to offer to others. I only want to be peaceful and friendly. Amen.

Initial Adjustments

Sunday

"Whoever cares for the poor lends to the LORD,
who will pay back the sum in full" (Proverbs 19:17).

Seek God in the poor. Some students at your university will not
have the same financial means as you. Perhaps they do not have the
latest and greatest technologies or perhaps their clothes are older, boring, and outdated. If a classmate asks to borrow something of yours,
imagine that person is Jesus. What would you say to him or her then?
Can you share what you have? When you do, that is pleasing to God.
When you look into the eyes of the poor, you will see God there. The
Lord knows all that you do, say, and give. Whatever you offer, do it
with much kindness and generosity. That will be pleasing to the Lord.
In what way can you give to the less fortunate on your campus or in
your community?

Dear God,

Help me to see you in my classmates. Enable me to find you
in the less fortunate I encounter in my travels. Allow me
to share what I have. Make my heart malleable and caring,
like yours, dear Lord. Amen.

Monday

"Jesus said to them, 'I am the bread of life;
whoever comes to me will never hunger, and
whoever believes in me will never thirst'" (John 6:35).

Care for your body and soul. Refuel your body with nutritious food
and drink plenty of water so you can think properly and focus in class.
Get some form of exercise each day to keep your body strong. For some,

that could happen during training for a sport; for others that might be a walk around campus or a visit to the gym. While it is essential to take care of yourself physically, God wants you to pray every day to keep your soul healthy and holy. While you are walking to class, can you eliminate useless or random thoughts that fill your head and replace them with loving contemplations for God? What are some ways that you can take care of your body and soul? Nourish your soul with the word of the Lord. Then you will be filled and overflowing with God's goodness. How will you pray today?

Dear God,

Fill my head and heart with loving thoughts of you.
Keep me well physically, mentally, and spiritually
so that I can serve you. Amen.

Tuesday

"Do not be friendly with hotheads, nor associate with the wrathful, lest you learn their ways, and become ensnared" (Proverbs 22:24–25).

Choose the path of righteousness. Do you know grumpy people? Walk away from argumentative students with hidden agendas. Surround yourself with people who worship, honor, and love God. Where can you find these students? Maybe you can participate in your school's church services or become involved in a center for spirituality at your university. Seek to grow in knowledge of God with your campus community by encouraging each other to build your relationship with the Lord. Perhaps there is a Newman Center that hosts social events, dinner meetings, retreats, and conferences stimulating your connection with God.

Dear God,

Fill me with the Holy Spirit and enlighten me with the
courage to avoid quarrelsome and confrontational people
who live in my dorm and attend class with me. Do not let
them misinterpret my kindness and compassion as a sign of
acceptance of their rude and brash behaviors. Let me stand as

an example of goodness for them to emulate. Let me be the
one they admire. Amen.

Wednesday

"Do not fear: I am with you; do not be anxious:
I am your God. I will strengthen you, I will help you,
I will uphold you with my victorious right hand"
(Isaiah 41:10).

Give your anxieties to God. Do you ever feel like everyone else is
handling the assignments, projects, and the daily workload except for
you? Have you ever felt that your classmates are smarter? God gave
you a magnificent mind to enable you to do anything. Instead of suc-
cumbing to the pressures of school, make a list of ways to include God
in your life to combat your stress today. A saint who endured anxiety
was Kateri Tekakwitha of Auriesville, New York. She was a Mohawk
Indian, adopted by relatives. Kateri experienced hostility from her tribe
because of her faith. Yet she established Native American ministries in
Catholic Churches throughout the nation. Her copious accomplishments resulted because of her love for and trust in God.

Dear God,

Strengthen me and allow me to accomplish the tasks that
have been set before me. Calm me with your love and lessen
my fears and apprehensions. With you by my side, I can do
anything. Amen.

Thursday

"Jesus looked at them and said, 'For human beings
this is impossible, but for God all things are possible'"
(Matthew 19:26).

Turn to God. Do you second-guess your curriculum? Are you overwhelmed with the requirements? When you review your schedule and
contemplate the work, what can you do to eliminate your misgivings?
What tasks are you faced with this week that appeal to you? Can you
focus on the positive in your classes and activities and pray about any

negative experiences you might have had? Give all of your reservations to God. Open your Bible and read God's Word. Shut out the world and make time to talk to God. Can you find a place of solitude on campus where you can pray and trust that God will help you sort out the mind-boggling issues that weigh you down?

Dear God,

Strengthen me and give me the stamina to continue my schoolwork. Expand my mind to understand so that I can do everything that is required of me. I don't want to let my parents, professors, and advisor down. Help me with my workload so that I can learn and grow. Amen.

Friday/Saturday

"If at Ephesus I fought with beasts, so to speak, what benefit was it to me? If the dead are not raised: 'Let us eat and drink, for tomorrow we die.' Do not be led astray: Bad company corrupts good morals" (1 Corinthians 15:32–33).

Align yourself with people who love God. Have you been invited to parties this weekend? Surround yourself with respectable students who spend their time productively getting to know and serve God. Do you know students who share your values? Can you socialize with them? What activities can you do with them this weekend? Perhaps you can opt for community service projects together as a form of socialization and service to God. Katharine Drexel, a Philadelphia, Pennsylvania, native, dedicated herself to the needs of oppressed indigenous peoples of the Americas and African Americans. She was an advocate of racial tolerance with efforts to attain quality education for everyone. She is the patron saint of racial justice and of philanthropists. How can this blessed saint invoke your interest for a dynamic way to spend your weekend?

Dear God,

Show me the path of righteousness; keep me on course. I trust in your plan for me, dear Lord. Amen.

Fitting In

Sunday

"The lamp of the body is the eye. If your eye is sound,
your whole body will be filled with light; but if your eye
is bad, your whole body will be in darkness. And if the
light in you is darkness, how great will the darkness be"
(Matthew 6:22–23).

Pray bad thoughts away. Have you ever caught yourself in a bulk of
negative thoughts? Maybe you worry about home or why your professor
hasn't posted your grades. Whenever undesirable thoughts cloud your
life, chase them away with prayer. Do not allow them the opportunity
to take root. Ask God to keep you wholesome, truthful, and genuine.
How can you fill your head and heart with loving thoughts of goodness for your classmates, professors, and family? Could a community
service project shine God's light in your life? Perhaps you could begin
by praying more frequently. Then you are brightening your world and
pleasing the Lord. Your first priority on earth is to get to heaven.

Dear God,

Please, Lord, fill me with loving thoughts of you. Thank you
for helping me to reach the halfway point in the semester.
Amen.

Monday

"For we do not have a high priest who is unable to sympathize with our weaknesses, but one who has similarly been tested in every way, yet without sin. So let us confidently approach the throne of grace to receive mercy and to find grace for timely help" (Hebrews 4:15–16).

Mistakes happen, for they are a universal part of life. Throughout your development in college, you will be faced with many decisions. How can you make better choices? Your professors understand that you will make mistakes; it's a part of your learning curve. What was your last mistake, and what did you learn from it? Failures, and the way you deal with them, could be the key to your future success. Learn from your blunders to become stronger and more capable of doing the work God intended for you.

Dear God,

Help me to accept, learn, and grow from my mistakes. Dear Lord, I am sorry for my faults; do not let me repeat them. Amen.

Tuesday

"Every word of God is tested; he is a shield
to those who take refuge in him" (Proverbs 30:5).

God keeps his promises. Have you ever made a promise to a friend and then broke it? Maybe you had a change of heart in a relationship that you thought would work out but didn't. Perhaps someone broke a promise to you and shattered your dreams. Facing a negative truth requires maturity to admit and want to correct. Reflect on your personality traits and consider the ones you have beautifully mastered. How can you exemplify them to work on other aspects of your character? Are there negative aspects regarding your personality that you struggle to admit, accept, or change? How will you face the truth about your vulnerabilities? During this humbling transformation, seek refuge in the Lord. Call out to God and take refuge in his love.

Dear God,

Open my ears to hear the truths that surround me. Hold my heart and comfort me as I work on self-improvement. Give me the strength and stamina to endure it. Help me to mature, accept, and transform into a wiser and a more amicable human being. Amen.

Wednesday

"But many who are first will be last, and the last will be first" (Matthew 19:30).

Be concerned with how God sees you. Do you worry about what to wear, wanting classmates to admire your awesome fashions? Maybe you overspend to make purchases you don't need just to be accepted by certain classmates. Do you buy designer clothes and dress to impress? Do you use profanities to be cool? Do you drink at parties to fit in? Do you know students who compromise their values and morals just to be popular? Do not put stock in what others think about you because it won't get you anywhere. Instead, focus on pleasing God and care what he thinks about you. Many students who appear to be the best in school now might diminish in popularity later on, while those who seem inconsequential could be the leaders of tomorrow.

Dear God,

Teach me how to be a good student and to care more about my education than fitting in with a popular crowd on campus. I truly care what you think of me. Do not let me settle for something less than I deserve. I do not want to compromise my values. Amen.

Thursday

"We who are strong ought to put up with the failings of the weak and not to please ourselves; let each of us please our neighbor for the good, for building up" (Romans 15:1–2).

Care for your neighbor. If you are strong, tolerate the shortcomings of the weak. Build up your neighbor. If someone is being harassed, intercede even if it is not convenient. If a classmate is carrying a heavy load, be supportive and offer assistance. Saint Marianne Cope devoted her life to caring for people. She opened and ran a school and two hospitals, and when she was asked to care for lepers in Molokai, Hawaii, she did it gladly. Have you ever ignored someone who needed care because you were busy? What are some ways you can spread God's love to your neighbor? Think about times in the past when you received help and appreciated it. How can you be more open to reaching out to others in your community today?

Dear God,

Call my attention to the people in need of my help, Lord.
Work through me to care for them the way you would.
Teach me compassion and patience. Amen.

Friday/Saturday

"Have mercy on me, God, have mercy on me. In you I seek refuge. In the shadow of your wings I seek refuge till harm pass by" (Psalm 57:2).

Stay the course with God. Have you ever driven to a place that you previously visited yet doubted your sense of direction along the way? Maybe the road looked different, or the landmarks had changed, making you feel lost. Do you remember how happy you felt when you finally arrived at the correct destination? Perhaps you needed positive reinforcement en route confirming that you were on the right path. As you plod along on your college journey, ask God to keep you on course. Can you ask God for indicators that guide you in the right direction? He knows how difficult your classes are. Give your troubled heart to God for he knows the true depth of your perseverance. What can you do today to augment your belief that God will help you navigate your way through college? Continue to trust in God that he will fulfill his purpose for you. Be patient. Everything will come together on God's terms, not yours.

Dear God,

I am eager to know if I am on the right course.
Teach me patience, Lord. Amen.

The Plunge

Sunday

> "Better is one handful with tranquility than two
>   with toil and a chase after wind!" (Ecclesiastes 4:6).

Seek rest in God's love. Prioritize everything that you must do. Are there any guest lectures or exhibits at your university this week? Does your college bookstore host author book signings? Untangle the chaos from your schedule by trying to organize it all: clubs, organizations, sports, and classes. If you cannot attend all of the activities this week, can you select which ones will benefit you the most? Make responsible choices when you manage your time so that you can take advantage of every worthwhile opportunity. Doing things indiscriminately is like trying to catch the wind. It will be exhausting and you will not have anything to show for it. How will you plan for rest and prayer in your busy week? What ways will you ensure that God makes your list?

> Dear God,
>
> You chose this path for me and I want to please you in everything I do. Bless my organizational skills. Give me the insight that I need to prioritize my work and functions and carry them through in a responsible manner. Amen.

Monday

> "Wait eagerly for the LORD, and keep his way;
>   he will raise you up to inherit the earth;
>   you will see when the wicked are cut off" (Psalm 37:34).

Avoid pitfalls by believing in God. Focus on your work because God put it in your path for a reason. He wants you to trust in him. God has a very important plan for you and at just the right moment, he will reveal it to you. Plod along steadily, be patient, and have faith in the Lord. When Saint Peter Damian was a college student, he had to overcome sinful temptations through prayer, fasting, and searching for God in his life. This ultimately led him to become the master of his spiritual life. In 1823, this Italian professor became known as a doctor of the Church. How can you maintain your faith in God and eliminate distractions? How will you put God first in your life today?

Dear God,

Help me to find satisfaction with what I am doing.
Keep diversions away from me. Be the center of my life
so that I may lead a virtuous life. I love you, Lord.

Tuesday

"Consider how he endured such opposition from sinners,
in order that you may not grow weary and lose heart....
So strengthen your drooping hands and your weak knees"
(Hebrews 12:3, 12).

Ask God for help. What projects, proposals, and presentations are you working on this week? Ask Jesus to fortify your body and mind to enable you to do well as you compile documents and data. Your thoughts and feelings are not unusual. Jesus was fully human and felt similar emotions. If you should trip or fall during your college journey, remember that Jesus stumbled three times on his way to Calvary. Each time he got up and kept going despite his suffering. What are you experiencing at school? What can you do to accept and live with others today? When Jesus became discouraged with the agony of his crucifixion, he turned to God and cried out to him. How will you ask for God's help?

Dear God,

I call out to you for help in dealing with my views and
sentiments. Remove any distractions so that I can focus
on my work and learn. Please help me, dear Lord. Amen.

Wednesday

"Those who disregard discipline hate themselves, but those
who heed reproof acquire understanding" (Proverbs 15:32).

Open your mind and heart to hear. Have you ever been stuck on
a homework problem, unable to figure it out? After you spot an error,
the answer seems obvious and easy to fix. Perhaps you stared at a map
and could not make sense of it. Or maybe you read a new chapter in a
textbook and could not understand it. It's frustrating to do something
repeatedly with little or no progress. Does this ever happen to you?
Listening to advice—whether it is from a teacher, mentor, or roommate—can be tough because "your way" might seem better. God put
these people in your path to help you learn and grow. What can you
do today to be more open to accepting information and feedback
from others?

Dear God,

Open my heart to acquiescing friendly advice and
recommendations. I know that by being more accepting it
could help me to prosper and become wiser. I am here to
learn, Lord. Teach me to be a good student. I ask this in your
sweet and holy name. Amen.

Thursday

"The person who is trustworthy in very small matters is also
trustworthy in great ones; and the person who is dishonest
in very small matters is also dishonest in great ones. If
therefore, you are not trustworthy with dishonest wealth,
who will trust you with true wealth?" (Luke 16:10–11).

Honesty begets morality. When you notice students in your dorm
being pleasant to each other, doing favors for one another, being helpful,
acting responsibly, can you befriend them? Do these students gather in
the lounges and include you in their discussions? When you observe
classmates who are authentically nice, they are typically trustworthy
people. How can you surround yourself with people like this? God

reminds his followers to always be loving and honest, even in little ways. He will reward you with greater opportunities and entrust you to the riches of heaven.

Dear God,

Surround me with honest people so that I can align myself with them. I want to be their lab partners, study-mates, and friends. Help me to identify sincere classmates who look out for my best interest. Guide me to the right people, dear Lord. Thank you for keeping me in your grace. Amen.

Friday/Saturday

"Though distress and anguish come upon me,
    your commandments are my delight" (Psalm 119:143).

God will give you strength. When the weekend arrives, it is natural to want to blow off steam from a rough week of classes. You might need some down time after working on difficult assignments, lengthy projects, and drafting essays. It is important to balance your workload with recreational activities. Who will you hang out with and what will you do? What worthwhile events could you participate in that would be fun and pleasing to God? You will be filled with abundant joy when you realize you are doing the right thing by gratifying God. In 1827, Saint Rose Philippine Duchesne created a new house of the Sacred Heart Society in Missouri, where she also founded an orphanage, a parish school, a school for Native Americans, a boarding academy, and spent much of her time nursing the sick. Her energy and ideas were exceptional. She is known as the saint who always prayed.

Dear God,

Surround me with the right group of people to spend my weekend with. Keep me vibrant as I thrive to keep you at the top of my priority list. Amen.

Personalities

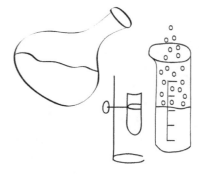

Sunday

"Good and upright is the LORD, therefore he shows sinners the way. He guides the humble in righteousness, and teaches the humble his way. All the paths of the LORD are mercy and truth toward those who honor his covenant and decrees" (Psalm 25:8–10).

God is kind and merciful. Often people learn their best lessons through mistakes they have made. It happens in laboratories where scientists try to make one thing but end up making something else with a more useful purpose. Penicillin was invented this way. Some mistakes are good. If you have made a mistake, don't worry for the Lord is with you. If you sin and are truly sorry for your sins, remember that God is forgiving and he can get you back on track. How can you show him that you mean what you say? What can you do to get back into God's special graces? God teaches with unconditional love and will never give up on you.

Dear God,

Thank you for being a kind and merciful Lord. Accept my remorse for the transgressions I have made against you. Please forgive me and help me to start over and do better. Amen.

Monday

"You have heard that it was said, 'You shall love your neighbor and hate your enemy.' But I say to you, love your enemies, and pray for those who persecute you, that you may be children of your heavenly Father, for he makes his sun rise on the bad and the good, and causes rain to fall on the just and the unjust" (Matthew 5:43–45).

Replace negative thoughts with prayer. Do you have classmates you truly admire? What characteristics are particularly attractive? There are certainly annoying students in every school who say unkind words. When harsh words are spoken, say a prayer. When misunderstandings and arguments ensue, Jesus says to act with love. It is the foundation of your faith that God is love and is there for everyone. When you pray for your enemies, you become more like God. Reflect on God's mercies in your life. How can you change?

> Dear God,
>
> Fill my heart with compassion for (_____) and help me to understand what he/she might be struggling with. Help me to forgive just as you forgave your enemies when you hung on the cross. Amen.

Tuesday

> "Therefore I tell you, all that you ask for in prayer, believe that you will receive it and it shall be yours. When you stand to pray, forgive anyone against whom you have a grievance, so that your heavenly Father may in turn forgive you your transgressions" (Mark 11:24–25).

Allow God to work through you. What do you ask of God? Do you ask him to bless you with many friends, good grades, or enlightenment and understanding? Perhaps you ask him to safeguard you as you walk across campus after a late night while studying in the library. When you request something of God, believe that you will receive what you ask for. If you do, God will give it to you. Additionally, try to be forgiving; then God will grant clemency for your iniquities. When you are forgiving, you will be free of bitterness, resentment, and grudges that can keep you from that special closeness with God.

> Dear God,
>
> Instill in me a forgiving heart, filled with your grace and endless love. Transform me, Lord, and work through me to be more kind, loving, and merciful. Amen.

Wednesday

"A wicked person desires the catch of evil people,
  but the root of the righteous will bear fruit" (Proverbs 12:12).

God is generous. You will meet a variety of people during your university experience. Some will come from wealthier families and be better dressed than you. They might take lavish vacations, and be well-connected socially with better opportunities. Some students will be smarter and get higher grades. Celebrate their good fortune. Recall the many gifts and talents that God has given to you. Stop and reflect on them. Has God brought many wonderful people into your life at school: friends, professors, tutors, or coaches? Who has been especially caring? What are some opportunities God has given to you this semester? Reflect on them for a few moments. It is feasible that other students crave what you have, your relationships, and aptitude. How can you show God your appreciation for all he has given to you?

Dear God.

Make my heart content with the many blessings you have showered me with over the years. You are such a kind and generous God. Thank you for all you have given to me.
I love you, sweet and generous Lord. Amen.

Thursday

"Deceit is in the heart of those who plot evil,
  but those who counsel peace have joy" (Proverbs 12:20).

Opt to be a peacemaker. In your stress-filled world, step back for a moment to remember that you have the Holy Spirit within you. Invoke the Spirit to bring composure, kind words, and loving thoughts to mind to quell tense situations. Invite the Holy Spirit to fill you with grace to promote peacefulness. Then, you can move on with a clear conscience and enjoy contentment by doing the right thing. Focus on being respectable. Keep love, peace, and joy in your heart because then there won't be any room for anything but true happiness. Mother Teresa advised to keep the joy of God in your heart and to give this contentment to others. She promoted this philosophy by giving her heart to Jesus.

Dear God,

Hold my heart in your hands, allowing all that is good and loving to enter it. Fill me with your grace and guide me down the path of righteousness. I only want to do what is pleasing to you, Lord. I will honor you all of the days of my life. I love you. Amen.

Friday/Saturday

"No trial has come to you but what is human. God is faithful and will not let you be tried beyond your strength; but with the trial he will also provide a way out, so that you may be able to bear it"(1 Corinthians 10:13).

God will not allow you to be tested beyond your limits. Are you tempted to take more than eighteen credit hours next semester because so many classes look interesting? Perhaps you are contemplating joining more organizations, clubs, or activities. Your temptations are similar to what other students experience. Through those challenges, what can you do to stay true to yourself and God? Remember that God is the most powerful force on heaven and earth. Call upon the powers of the Holy Spirit to guide you through your decisions.

Dear God,

Keep me strong as I stand up to temptations that surround me on campus. My time is precious and I want to try to do everything. Don't let me have regrets. Be with me, sweet and loving Lord, and keep me on the right path. Amen.

Homecoming/ Parents' Weekend

Sunday

"No foul language should come out of your mouths, but only such as is good for needed edification, that it may impart grace to those who hear" (Ephesians 4:29).

Speak the love language; it delights God. There are students on your campus who will go to extreme lengths to excel. You don't have to take precarious measures to outshine your classmates because you have the Holy Spirit within you enabling you to be the very best. Let everything you say be helpful so that your words will be encouraging to those who listen. How can you entwine your words with love? What words of encouragement can you offer your friends, and how do you plan to speak lovingly to people, regardless of whether or not they deserve it this week?

Dear God,

Bless me with compassion for all people I meet, whether or not they deserve my kindness. Let me draw from an endless well of love for everyone I encounter today, tomorrow, and always. Let me use Jesus as my role model. I love you, Lord. Amen.

Monday

"Therefore, since we are surrounded by so great a cloud of witnesses, let us rid ourselves of every burden and sin that clings to us and persevere in running the race that lies before us while keeping our eyes fixed on Jesus, the leader and perfecter of faith. For the sake of the joy that lay before him he endured the cross, despising its shame, and has taken his seat at the right of the throne of God. Consider how he endured such opposition from sinners, in order that you may not grow weary and lose heart" (Hebrews 12:1–3).

Avoid sin. Strip off the weight that slows you. Run with fortitude the race God has established while keeping your eyes on Jesus. As you face the myriad decisions and pressures of today, what classes to attend, or projects to begin, how do you plan to stay focused on God? How will you avoid distractions that could derail you? Focus on Jesus and the suffering he endured during his crucifixion. Perhaps that will reinforce your drive and stamina to strive onward.

Dear God,

Fill my heart with love, kindness, and compassion.
Make me the best version of myself. Amen.

Tuesday

"When cares increase within me, your comfort gives me joy" (Psalm 94:19).

Focus on God. Have you recently reviewed your course syllabus and panicked because of the many required obligations you face? Are you satisfied with your current grades? Are your professors laid back and easy to talk to and understand? It is normal to question yourself, but remember to make God your focal point. How will you focus in on God? He is the one who will bring you comfort and renewed spiritual growth. When can you spend quality time talking to God today? Schedule an appointment with him. As long as you place God first in your life, everything else will fall miraculously into place. Saint Mother Théodore Guérin put God first in her life by becoming a nun and caring for the poor, sick, and dying. She left her home in France and traveled to America where she founded the Sisters of Providence in Indiana. She also founded numerous schools, including Saint Mary-of-the-Woods College.

Dear God,

Guide me as I deal with my infallibilities. Clear any irrational thoughts and replace them with tranquility, love, and peace. I humbly ask this of you, dear Lord. Amen.

Wednesday

"Blessed are those who trust in the LORD;
the LORD will be their trust" (Jeremiah 17:7).

Get to know God best. Some people depend on music to put them in a good mood. They plug in their Mp3 Player, scroll to an upbeat song, and crank it up. Others rely on exercise to elevate their spirits. When they get stressed, they head to the gym and lift weights or run on the treadmill. Soon, endorphins are flowing and their stress has melted away. Some students eat junk food or chocolate. What coping strategies work for you? Whenever you feel anxiety, could you pray? God wants you to know him so well that it becomes second nature to trust in him. The best way to come to know God is through prayer and spiritual reflection, reading the Bible, and service to the less fortunate. Tune out the world and tune in to God, the best stress reliever.

Dear God,

Teach me to release the stress of school to you and spend quality time getting to know you. I want to know, love, serve, and adore you. Amen.

Thursday

"Look, God is exalted in his power.
What teacher is there like him?" (Job 36:22).

Always put God first in your life. Did you have a favorite teacher in high school? You will encounter many wonderful professors, teacher's assistants, and tutors while you are in college. Some of the best educators also turn out to be awesome mentors. Learn as much as you can from them because after graduation, your paths may not cross again. The one true teacher to keep in your life is God, the constant one you can always depend upon. He will not leave you after you graduate. God was with you when you were born, he never left your side throughout your childhood, and he is surely with you now in college. What are a few things you can do to put God first in your life today? How can you promote learning more about God?

Dear God,

Help me to remember to put you first in my life. You are truly the best teacher I have. With you I can conquer anything. I love you more than anything in the world. You are my world. I revolve around you. Amen.

Friday/Saturday

"To eat too much honey is not good;
  nor to seek honor after honor.
A city breached and left defenseless
are those who do not control their temper"
(Proverbs 25:27–28).

Ask God for guidance. During homecoming weekend many activities are planned: football games, tailgate parties, campus tours, ice cream socials, comedy spots, parades, fireworks, and concerts. When can you fit homework into your busy schedule? Perhaps your parents are visiting for the first time and your excitement to see them prevents you from studying. There will be many occasions for you to overindulge while you are in college. What do you do to exercise self-control? How do you know when to stay and when to walk away? One friend you can always turn to is Jesus. Call out to him; ask for his companionship and direction. He is always with you and he longs to hear from you. When will you talk to Jesus this weekend?

Dear God,

Teach me to maintain self-control at school. There are many opportunities to overindulge during homecoming weekend. Help me to stay strong and put you first in my life. Amen.

Stay the Course

Sunday

"Your reign is a reign for all ages, your dominion for all
generations. The LORD is trustworthy in all his words,
and loving in all his works. The LORD supports all
who are falling and raises up all who are bowed down.
The eyes of all look hopefully to you; you give them
their food in due season" (Psalm 145:13–15).

Call out to God. During midterm exams, many students feel stressed
out and overwhelmed. Are you feeling this way? Call out to the Lord.
He is there waiting to hold you in his loving arms, to nourish, and
protect you. Ask him to help you prepare for your tests, papers, and
presentations and keep focused while doing your best. What can you
do today to reinforce your confidence in God?

Dear God,

Make me flexible so I can do anything you ask. Give me the
courage to bend and believe that I will not break. All that I
do is for you. I offer to you my studies and the way I suffer
through classes, homework, and exams. I know that storms
may blow through my life while I am in college, and I ask
that you give me the courage to weather through all of them.
Amen.

Monday

"In the morning you will say, 'Would that it were evening!'
and in the evening you will say, 'Would that it were morning!'
because of the dread that your heart must feel and the sight
that your eyes must see" (Deuteronomy 28:67).

You are not alone. It is possible to be overwhelmed with a myriad
of exam questions. So much is riding on the tests. Do you have test

anxiety? Do not panic! Take in a deep breath and close your eyes, letting the breath out slowly while thinking about Jesus. Remember that the Holy Spirit is in you. You are not taking the test alone. Ask the Holy Spirit to enlighten you. The Spirit can lessen your apprehensions and fears. Ask the Holy Spirit to help you recall everything that you have studied; to clear your mind of the clutter and bring into focus everything you have learned in school. Take a moment to reflect on all of the blessings that God has given to you. When your exams are over, how can you offer thanksgiving to God for helping you through this difficulty.

Dear God,

Be with me as I take my midterm exams. Erase the confusion in my mind and leave all of the knowledge that I have been acquiring at this university. Help me to do well. Amen.

Tuesday

"False scales are an abomination to the LORD,
  but an honest weight, his delight" (Proverbs 11:1).

Always be truthful. Do you know someone who is dishonest or omits information to their professors? Omission is a form of dishonesty. Reflect on times in the past when someone lied to you. How did you get over that? After a heartfelt introspection, can you be truthful about your own feelings, emotions, and spirituality? God wants you to be honest with everyone. It pleases God to know that you are living by his rules. God will bless you and keep you in his good graces. How will you live in truthfulness today? Can you start by examining your conscience and vowing to be truthful with yourself?

Dear God,

Help me to have an honest heart. While it is tempting to tell a little white lie, I realize it pleases you when I am truthful. Teach me how to be honest all of the time and free me from the grasp of dishonesty. I want my intentions to be as pure as my actions. Amen.

Wednesday

"Instruct the wise, and they become still wiser;
teach the just, and they advance in learning" (Proverbs 9:9).

Never stop learning. Athletes constantly strive to do their best, putting forth one hundred percent each and every time they are challenged. They keep their bodies fortified by eating healthy foods, exercising, and training persistently. You are an athlete of knowledge, therefore, think and drill like one. To keep your mind as sharp as possible, other areas of your life must also be in order, including your spirituality. How will you embrace God and get to know him better? The more you learn about God, the smarter you will become.

Dear God,

Empower me with the ability to learn as much as I possibly can today. The semester is slipping away and midterm exams are upon me. Fill my head with as much knowledge as my brain can comprehend. Pour love into my heart so that I can use all that I have learned. Teach me how to give it all away to enlighten others and use me as an instrument so that I can do your work to the best of my abilities. Amen.

Thursday

"When you pass through waters, I will be with you; through rivers, you shall not be swept away. When you walk through fire, you shall not be burned, nor will flames consume you. For I, the LORD, am your God, the Holy One of Israel, your savior. I give Egypt as ransom for you, Ethiopia and Seba in exchange for you" (Isaiah 43:2–3).

You and God will get through anything together. It is difficult to prepare for and take exams and to give presentations and papers. Though these moments may feel burdensome, it is important to recognize that learning is a blessing granted to us by God. College life is an experience that many in the world will never have. Take a break and go for a walk to enjoy the beauty of autumn, the crispness of the air and the colorful trees. There are many healthy options for dealing with pre-examination pressure. When you are struggling through these difficult situations, remember that God is beside you and the Holy Spirit is in you. How will you rely on your faith to help you through this demanding period?

Dear God,

Fill me with your love as I get through the last of midterm exams, presentations, and reports. Enlighten me and help me to stay well. Amen.

Friday/Saturday

"I say, then: live by the Spirit and you will certainly not gratify the desire of the flesh. For the flesh has desires against the Spirit, and the Spirit against the flesh; these are opposed to each other, so that you may not do what you want" (Galatians 5:16–17).

Let the Holy Spirit guide your life. As you make weekend plans, think about the depth of God's love for you. While you carve Halloween pumpkins, go hiking, or attend a football game, remember that these pleasurable afternoon events are a treat the Lord wants you to enjoy as a part of your college experience. Allow the Holy Spirit to intervene as you select your activities and the crowd you want to hang out with. When you struggle to decide between all of the happenings, ask the Holy Spirit to enable you to keep your convictions strong. Can you adapt and assimilate the Holy Spirit in making all future weekend plans? How will you do this?

Dear God,

Keep me safe as I absorb your love and delight in the treasures you have provided this weekend. Thank you for blessing me with so many gifts. Amen.

Acceptance

Sunday

"All scripture is inspired by God and is useful for teaching,
for refutation, for correction, and for training in righteousness,
so that one who belongs to God may be competent, equipped
for every good work" (2 Timothy 3:16–17).

To know God, read the Bible. Scripture teaches what is true and
helps you to realize what improvements you can make in your life. Is
everything OK in your life? You won't know for certain unless you
study the Bible. God uses Scripture to prepare and equip you to do
good works. Saint Bonaventure explains that reading and understanding Scripture leads to heaven. Jesus lights the way through his words,
and safe passage into heaven comes through Christ. Out of all of the
books that surround you at college, the one most vital to prepare
for your future is the Bible. Can you read it every day to ensure you
understand God's messages? Does your university have a Bible-study
group? Perhaps you could attend or create one. God made you for
community, that is to learn and pray with others. Would you benefit
from reading the Bible in a group setting?

Dear God,

Help me to understand the Scripture.
I want to be committed to live by your Word. Amen.

Monday

"Let us not grow tired of doing good, for in due time we shall
reap our harvest, if we do not give up. So then, while we have
the opportunity, let us do good to all, but especially to those
who belong to the family of the faith" (Galatians 6:9–10).

Do good deeds. At the right time you will reap a harvest of blessings if you do not give up. Do good deeds whenever the opportunity arises. It is difficult to do something nice for those who are unlovable. Do you know someone like that? God has placed ornery people in your life for a reason. They are like an onion, with layers that need to be peeled back, often making you cry. But in that process, joy will come. When you reach out to someone in love, your heart will be forever changed. Can you do that, knowing how happy it will make God?

Dear God,

Help me to be pleasant to insincere people who might appear undeserving. Make it easier for me to smile and offer kind gestures to cranky people who are annoying. They need my love the most. Amen.

Tuesday

"Since we have gifts that differ according to the grace given to us, let us exercise them: if prophecy, in proportion to the faith" (Romans 12:6).

What is your God-given talent? God has given you many different gifts for doing certain things well. Maybe you play a musical instrument or can sing, act, or dance. Do you have exceptional athletic abilities? Are you extraordinarily hospitable and sociable? What are your talents? God wants you to use them. If your talent is to serve, God wants you to do that. If your talent is to encourage others, God wants you to inspire everyone around you. Not to use your God-given talents is an offense to our Lord, and it robs others of your giftedness. How can you use your talents to serve God? Use your abilities to serve the Lord and it will be pleasing to him as long as it is done cheerfully and with much love.

Dear God,
What are my talents and how will I use them at school? I barely have enough time to work and study. Help me to recognize my abilities and use them wisely, humbly, and with much love. Amen.

Wednesday

"Hatred stirs up disputes, but love covers all offenses"
(Proverbs 10:12).

God teaches to love unconditionally. Universities are like a giant pot of stew made up of a lot of different ingredients: carrots, celery, peas, beans, potatoes, meat, mushrooms, wine, and spices. It's the variety of mixed components that makes it good. Similarly, universities draw into the academic environment diversity among its students and professors, which makes it interesting and good. With this mixture of differences comes an assortment of philosophies, cultures, morals, and values. Do you hold people's differences against them? How can you be more loving to people who have mixed opinions? Perhaps they can influence a new way for problem-solving in class. Is there an international club on campus you could join? Varied cultures could add the spice to your life that has been otherwise lacking. God loves you unconditionally, so love others the way God loves you: totally and completely with all of his heart and soul, even when you hurt him.

Dear God,

Help me to accept those people on my campus who are different. Enable me to see their unique beauty. Facilitate a loving relationship among us. Amen.

Thursday

"The stone the builders rejected has become the cornerstone"
(Psalm 118:22).

Differences are good. Builders reject stones because they are the wrong color or size, but God looks for uniqueness in every stone. It's a good thing that the world is full of different people; otherwise, life would be dull. How good would it be if the dining hall only served broth? How tiresome would it be if your campus only had one form of entertainment or one kind of innocuous elective? Differences allow for choices, which is essential on a college campus. Do you ever feel like you are different? Jesus was "different." Those who are different, take refuge in the Lord because God loves us for our differences and uniqueness. Do you know someone who is distinctive, and can you pray for that person? God knows that great things can be built from the rare and exclusive abilities that you are developing and fine-tuning at school.

Dear God,

Thank you for making me unique. I feel special because of my differences and I appreciate that because of those variations, I have much to offer the world. Amen.

Friday/Saturday

"Blessed are you when people hate you, and when they exclude and insult you, and denounce your name as evil on account of the Son of Man" (Luke 6:22).

Worship in community. Does your university have a center for spirituality or a Newman Center? It is important to surround yourself with people who believe in and celebrate the Lord and Savior. Perhaps you could participate in a faith-sharing or Bible-study group. This would give you an opportunity to connect with God in a safe environment where you will not be judged for worshiping God. When are you ridiculed or cursed because you believe in God? Know that he will bless you for it. Are you ever tempted to hide your faith in order to be accepted by some people? Stand up for what you believe in and remember that God is always with you, especially in times of trouble. Many blessings await you when people hate you, exclude you, mock you, and curse you because you believe in Jesus. Can you take a risk with God?

Dear God,

Empower me as I take a stand for you.
I love you, dear Lord.
No one can take that away. Amen.

Autumn Colors

Sunday

"Yes, if you call for intelligence, and to understanding raise
your voice; If you seek her like silver, and like hidden treasures
search her out, Then will you understand the fear of the LORD;
the knowledge of God you will find" (Proverbs 2:3–5).

God has a magnificent plan for you. He brought you to the school
you are attending and places particular people on your path for a
reason: professors, teaching assistants, advisors, lab partners, roommates, and tutors. God is preparing you for something wonderful in
your future. Ask God for enlightenment. Do you take advantage of
the opportunities that God has lined up for you? Sometimes, you have
to search for them as if you were looking for a buried treasure. Think
about missed opportunities that you let pass by. What can you do this
week to take full advantage of God's blessings and gifts for you? Trust
in the Lord's plan.

Dear God,

Grant me the wisdom I long for to enable me to understand
all that I must learn. Open my mind to absorb and digest this
wisdom. Grant me the knowledge I need to do your work,
whatever it is. I trust you. Amen.

Monday

"For I know well the plans I have in mind for you,
   says the LORD, plans for your welfare and not for woe,
   so as to give you a future of hope" (Jeremiah 29:11).

Have faith in God while you wait. How hard is it to wait for something good to happen? Have you ever tried to meet friends in a crowded mall or at a festival? Perhaps you had a prearranged meeting spot, but questioned it as time rolled by. With throngs of people to see around, it is understandable to be restless as you bide time. Waiting is difficult. You might feel as if you are not on the right path at school, or perhaps headed in the wrong direction. Do you question God with your destiny? When God created you, he had your purpose in his mind. He has mighty plans for you. How can you be faithful while you anticipate God to reveal his plan to you? What can you do today to make your wait more bearable?

Dear God,

I know you will find me amidst hordes of people, swallowed by distractions, and not let me be harmed. You are such an amazing God, categorically worth waiting for. Amen.

Tuesday

"His master said to him, 'Well done, my good and faithful servant. Since you were faithful in small matters, I will give you great responsibilities. Come, share your master's joy'" (Matthew 25:23).

God rewards your faithfulness. Have you ever noticed when you have proven yourself that you are entrusted with more notable responsibilities? Once you have proven yourself in class, your professor moves on to something more demanding because he believes you can progress to the next level of challenges. This also happens in musical performances, sports, and on your job. God will grant you more opportunities to serve him with even greater responsibilities. Do not fret over your ability to handle such tasks because God is always with you. You never work alone. If God wants you to have help, he will bring someone into your life to help you. How will you rise to the challenges God sets before you today?

Dear God,

Thank you for believing in me. I will strive to do my best and please you. Thank you for having such a wonderful master plan for my life. You have put me in the perfect place. I trust in you, dear Lord. Amen.

Wednesday

"Behold, you desire true sincerity;
  and secretly you teach me wisdom" (Psalm 51:8).

God knows the real you. Most students strive to "look good," appear intelligent, and impress their teachers and classmates. It might only be a façade attempting to fool others into thinking they know more than they really do. In class, can you focus your energy simply on learning? Outside of the classroom, can you focus on the Lord and Savior? How will you do that? Only God knows what is in your heart, because he made you. The one that you really need to please is God. His opinion is the most important. Ask God to help your outside appearances to match the true colors of your heart. Look for ways to be more genuinely you.

Dear God,

Humble me, Lord. Help me to stop trying to impress everyone around me. I do not care what other students think about me. Help me to focus on the truly important matters: pleasing you. Teach me how to stop looking at others and to do an intro-spection of myself. You are my ticket into heaven and my sole reward. Amen.

Thursday

"Jesus said to them in reply, 'Those who are healthy do not need a physician, but the sick do. I have not come to call the righteous to repentance but sinners" (Luke 5:31–32).

Jesus helps those in need. Does your school have a learning center for anxious students? Some are gifted with ease of study, while others have to work hard to get a high grade-point average. If necessary, do not be afraid to seek consult with the learning center or seek a tutor. Your professors do not expect you to be perfect; they know you will make mistakes because you are learning. You do not have to be supremely ideal for Jesus to love you. He wants to help the brokenhearted and disadvantaged, and desires all to become their true selves. Self-righteousness and pride hinder Jesus from entering our hearts, but humility and love open the door to our Lord. If Jesus was your tutor, what problem would you give to him today? What would Jesus ask you to improve upon? What are some changes that you could make today that would bring you closer to the Lord?

Dear God,

Shed your light on me to heal my wounds and help me to find my way through school. Illuminate the way and I will follow. I ask this in your sweet name. Amen.

Friday/Saturday

"Teach us to count our days aright,
that we may gain wisdom of heart" (Psalm 90:12).

Life is short; use your time wisely. Once the weekend arrives, there are many different ways to spend it. Perhaps the time is right to take a road trip to explore a new area or reconnect with other friends. It is tempting to put off assignments. You might think you have oodles of time to accomplish tasks and get your life in order. Do you know any procrastinators? Re-evaluate your end-of-semester goals to see if you are on target. Can you schedule time each day for prayerful reflection and reading the Bible? Studying your Bible is as important as preparing for your classes. Ask God to direct you on the course he wants you to take. God will energize and strengthen you in order to do his work. Always trust in God.

Dear God,

Help me to be productive with my precious time. There is so much I need to accomplish before graduation. Help me to enjoy college because the joy is not waiting at my graduation ceremony, but in the journey to get there. Thank you, Lord, for these experiences. Amen.

November

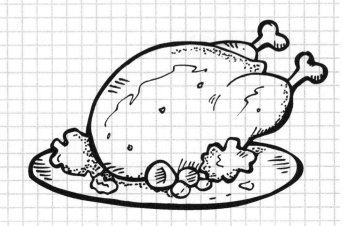

Preparing for the Winter Chill

Sunday

"As for me, to be near God is my good, to make the Lord God my refuge. I shall declare all your works in the gates of daughter Zion" (Psalm 73:28).

Give your qualms to God. Are you disillusioned about your future? Do you question your capabilities of working in the profession you are studying? If you feel this way, pray. Prayer draws you close to God. Take shelter in God's love when you doubt your courses, your future, or friends. Prayer can reinforce that you are exactly where you are meant to be. On the feast of All Saints Day, can you pray to saints who are the most like you? How will you honor the martyrs of sainthood? Surround yourself with faithful students who aspire to achieve greatness likened to those qualities of the saints you admire. The saints all had diverse personalities; some were fierce in battle, others were shy and reserved. What saint can you best relate to?

Dear God,

As I approach the end of this semester, I am thankful that you have been with me every step of the way. Thank you for your love and constant protection. Amen.

Monday

> Be "strengthened with every power, in accord with his glorious might, for all endurance and patience, with joy" (Colossians 1:11).

God is always with you. Develop good organizational skills now so that you know what needs to be done and when it is due. This will help you stay on target and not fall behind in your work. It is not easy juggling a heavy course load and participating in clubs or sports. A lot of pressure is on you to succeed. Do not focus all of your energies on school. Spend time with God in prayer. When God's power begins to work in you, where will you draw endurance and patience so that you can do his work? How will you get through any chaos in your life? Always remember that you are not alone in your situation.

> Dear God,
>
> Help me see you amidst the sea of confusion and obligations of school. Help me, Lord, to focus on you and be assured that everything will be OK. I trust in your plan for me, even though I do not know what it is. Amen.

Tuesday

> "Do not be afraid of sudden terror, of the ruin of the wicked when it comes; For the LORD will be your confidence, and will keep your foot from the snare" (Proverbs 3:25–26).

God will give you what you need. When your professor announces a pop quiz or students ridicule you for going to church, do not panic. The Lord is with you. He will not let anyone bring harm to you. Ask God to quell your nerves. Everything will be all right as long as you give it to God. If a storm should blow through your school today, what can you do to rid your trepidations? Can you think of Jesus hanging on the cross, imagining the suffering he endured? Find the calm in every storm by allowing God to embrace you and fill you with peace, love, and joy. Always remember that God will provide.

Dear God,

Shelter me from harm as it drifts nearby. Keep me strong as I continue on the path of righteousness. There is a place for you in my heart and in my life. Amen.

Wednesday

"Am I now currying favor with human beings or God? Or am I seeking to please people? If I were still trying to please people, I would not be a slave of Christ" (Galatians 1:10).

Always choose God. It's nice to do favors for friends. Maybe a classmate included you in their carpool to and from your hometown. Perhaps someone helped edit your paper or invited you to a concert. What are some kindnesses you have extended to classmates? Sometimes friends can get you into trouble with your school or parents. Has anyone tried to persuade you to do something that was not in your best interest? It is human nature to seek approval from those around you, but it is essential to place God above all others. If there is a conflict between pleasing God and a classmate, always choose God. A true friend would never "test" your loyalty. What can you do today to let God know he is first in your life?

Dear God,

Remove the negative people from my life. Keep me strong when people test me. Bless me with serenity and lead me on the right path. Keep me in your good graces. Amen.

Thursday

"So submit yourselves to God. Resist the devil, and he will flee from you. Draw near to God, and he will draw near to you. Cleanse your hands, you sinners, and purify your hearts, you of two minds" (James 4:7–8).

Have a relationship with God. As you try to find your way through life, God will be near and keep you safe. For every situation in life that you face, God created someone who is an example of holiness and purity by satisfying their religious commitments. These people are on your campus; you may not know it, but you can feel it. It is evident in the way they carry themselves, their actions, principles, morals, and values. Think about individuals on your campus who are this way: a spiritual advisor, counselor, or campus minister. Can you surround yourself with them or people like them? What is their purpose, and how does it impact you?

Dear God,

Fortify me so that I can endure and plod ahead drawing nearer to you, dear Lord. Help me to identify the individuals you allowed to cross my path and to support me. You are so sweet and generous in your love and mercies for me. Amen.

Friday/Saturday

"For those who live according to the flesh are concerned with the things of the flesh, but those who live according to the spirit with the things of the spirit. The concern of the flesh is death, but the concern of the spirit is life and peace" (Romans 8:5–6).

Do not fall into a pattern of sinfulness. Are you considering attending a rave, frat, or sorority party this weekend? In making plans, how can you ensure that you will embrace all that is respectable, right, and pure? God gave you the freedom to follow your dreams and goals. What are they and what can you do this weekend to begin to fulfill them? Wherever you go and whatever you do, honor God first. Ask the Holy Spirit to empower you with all that is good and holy. Can you give the Holy Spirit control of your mind and heart to thwart temptations that surround you on campus? If you do this, you will be filled with peace.

Dear God,

Keep my eyes sharp, my mind alert, and my heart brimming with love. I ask this in your name, sweet Jesus. Amen.

Endurance

Sunday

"For whenever anyone bears the pain of unjust suffering
because of consciousness of God, that is a grace"
(1 Peter 2:19).

Give it to God. When anxious teens received acceptance letters from
colleges, many did not get into their favorite school. Some were accepted but could not afford tuition. These disappointments caused
dashed dreams due to no fault of their own. But they rose above it
and found another worthwhile college. God is pleased when you do
what is right and patiently endure unjust treatment. Have you had to
suffer unfairly? How did you bear it? Sometimes the only thing you
can modify in an unfair situation is to change your attitude toward
it. If you cannot change it, fix it, or ignore it, can you give it to God
and pray on it? Ask God to help carry your burden. God will carry it
so that you don't have to do it alone.

Dear God,

Thank you for helping me through my unfair situation and
for the patience to endure it and see it through. Thank you
for enabling me to trust in your master plan for me and
showing me the way to heaven. Amen.

Monday

> "And the king will say to them in reply, 'Amen, I say to you, whatever you did for one of these least brothers of mine, you did for me'" (Matthew 25:40).

You are a part of God's family. Most people are protective of their families. Whether you feel this way about your family at home or the new family you have established with your roommate, classmates, and friends, there is a connection bound by loyalty. If someone you care for were injured, it would impact you greatly. Each person on campus is part of God's family. Each student is precious to God, just as you are exceptional to your family and to God. Can you smile or offer a caring gesture to someone on your campus today? It is easy to be nice to people you like, but can you be cordial to someone you don't know or like?

Dear God,

Bless all of the people in your family that I may have hurt unintentionally. Pardon me and I will try harder to be kind and loving to everyone. I want to walk in your light. Amen.

Tuesday

> "If you forgive others their transgressions, your heavenly Father will forgive you. But if you do not forgive others, neither will your Father forgive your transgressions" (Matthew 6:14–15).

Forgive, let go, and move on. It can be difficult to excuse people who hurt you. However, it is mandatory if you want God to pardon your sins. Forgiveness does not mean that the hurt and disappointment does not exist; nevertheless, it is the first step in the healing process. Is it challenging for you to be compassionate? Forgiveness affords you the ability to move on with your life, to achieve your goals, and pursue your dreams. Do not let someone else's problems stifle you. Can you forgive someone today knowing it is pleasing to God and healing for you? The world is a wonderful place and God has glorious plans for you. Do not let the pain of transgressions stop you from living, loving, and learning. How can you become more forgiving in the future?

Dear God,
Teach me how to make my heart more forgiving and to accept the shortcomings of others. Teach me how to love others without conditions. I ask this of you, dear Lord. Amen.

Wednesday

"But it shall not be so among you. Rather, whoever wishes to be great among you shall be your servant" (Matthew 20:26).

Be a humble servant. Leadership roles could open up to you in college. Perhaps you could become a club president or volunteer as a student leader for your campus ministry program. Having leadership roles in college builds your résumé and will possibly impress future employers. Club presidents accept many responsibilities in order to carry out their roles successfully. Do you see yourself as a leader in some way? If you decide to lead or step up and help organize an event or club, can you emulate Jesus' leadership style? Jesus used his power to serve others. Do not adhere to your own agenda. How can you be a humble servant on your campus or faith community? How do you reach out to others in need by adhering to Jesus' philosophies?

Dear God,

Grant me the courage and wisdom to accept a leadership role at school. Teach me how to be a servant to other members of the organizations that I am involved in. Please, Lord, let me guide and manage the members with style and grace. Do not let power be my motivator. I want to be a wise and well-respected leader whom students admire and want to emulate. Amen.

Thursday

"They are renewed each morning—great is your faithfulness!" (Lamentations 3:23).

Ask God for a "do over." As sure as the sun rises and sets each day, you can count on God's love and mercy to be steadfast. When you start each new day, ask for God's forgiveness for wrongdoings with heartfelt contemplation. God is kind and merciful, and his unconditional love reigns in your heart. What can you do to be more Christ-like to your classmates? You are human, full of fragility, goodness, and capable of repair. Make today a good one because it is a gift from God. What are you doing with your talents and gifts that come from God. How will you make this day productive as a gift to God? In Anzio, Italy, in 1902, Maria Goretti was stabbed by a neighbor after he tried to rape her. She forgave him from her hospital bed before she died. She is the patroness of youth and for victims of rape. If you know someone who has been raped, encourage her to get professional help and pray to Saint Maria Goretti for intercession.

Dear God,
You are such a great and merciful Lord.
Enable me to be more like you. Amen.

Friday/Saturday

"This is the will of God, your holiness: that you refrain from
immorality, that each of you know how to acquire a wife for
himself in holiness and honor, not in lustful passion as do the
Gentiles who do not know God" (1 Thessalonians 4:3–5).

Give yourself wholly and completely to God. There are many opportunities for sexual encounters in college, but that is not what God wants for you. There are mixers, late-night parties, and overnight field trips. It is understandable to want to participate in some of these activities, but do not lose a part of yourself at them. Always keep your best interest in mind. Are you planning to engage in sex before marriage? Jesus said sex outside of marriages degrades what is holy and is damaging spiritually.

Dear God,

Help me to stay true to myself. Keep me strong so that I
stay focused and pure. Bless all of my relationships with the
people who are near and dear to my heart. Amen.

Preparation for the Final "Push"

Sunday

"You even joined in the sufferings of those in prison and joyfully accepted the confiscation of your property, knowing that you had a better and lasting possession" (Hebrews 10:34).

God does everything for a reason. You do not have to like the situation you are in at school. If you cannot change it, than accept it. Perhaps you can find comfort if you emphasize changing your attitude toward your struggle. Can you trust that God has a greater purpose for you? Perhaps then, being tested in certain circumstances might be easier to endure. Suffering through stress and studies are temporary. What can you do today to minimize the misery? How can you embrace this stage of your life? What blessing from God can you dwell on to get you through this difficulty?

Dear God,

Strengthen me, dear Lord, as I struggle through my studies and wrestle to maintain focus on all that is good and right in this world. Keep my motivation and concentration strong. Thank you for reminding me to pray today for I know that prayer builds resilience. With you at my side, I can do anything. Amen.

Monday

"Not that of ourselves we are qualified to take credit for
anything as coming from us; rather, our qualification comes
from God, who has indeed qualified us as ministers of a
new covenant, not of letter but of spirit; for the letter brings
death, but the Spirit gives life" (2 Corinthians 3:5–6).

Your competence is from God. He made you competent to be a
minister of a new covenant. Do not overanalyze your competence
because it is a gift from God. Are you complacent in your day-to-day
grind? Place your faith in God, and he will provide the optimism and
confidence necessary to enable you to do well in school so that some
day you can do his work. How will you do this? For now, you are
exactly where God wants you to be.

Dear God,

Quiet my restless heart. Remind me that I am where you want
me to be. Continue to provide the skills and abilities that I
need to carry out your plan. Help me to learn from moments
of discouragement how to be more determined and successful.
Show me how and teach me the way, Lord. I trust you. Amen.

Tuesday

"As a result, those who suffer in accord with God's will
hand their souls over to a faithful creator as they do good"
(1 Peter 4:19).

Suffering builds character. Is one particular class, perhaps math or
science, difficult for you? Problems can either strengthen you or wear
you down. Do not look at your problems as insurmountable obstacles.
Can you look at them in a different light, from another angle, and
embrace them? Suffering will enable you to grow if you allow God to
work within you. How will you let God work in you? Every time you
see a cross, think of Christ as he hung from it.

Dear God,

I humbly ask that you bless me with the confidence that I need to do your work. I spend hours studying, trying to understand and get good grades. I believe there is a very special plan for me. If I stay on the right track, with your guidance, I will reach the destination. Sometimes I get discouraged with schoolwork, but then I remember all you have given me, and I know you will continue to bless me. Thank you for always being there for me. Amen.

Wednesday

"All bitterness, fury, anger, shouting, and reviling must be removed from you, along with all malice. [And] be kind to one another, compassionate, forgiving one another as God has forgiven you in Christ" (Ephesians 4:31–32).

Be kind and forgiving. Be generous and compassionate to your classmates. How can you surround yourself with kind people on campus? Reflect on times when you were included in a caring group of students on campus that made you feel accepted and loved. Was it a group of tight-knit friends, community-service organizations, student government, a fraternity or sorority, spring break-out, etc.? Where do you feel most comfortable? What do you value at school? Recall all of the blessings God has given to you this semester and thank God for them all.

Dear God,

Bless with me peacefulness. Let my heart overflow with goodness and joy so that there is no room for maliciousness. Let me find value in every person I meet, overlooking their flaws to see their good qualities. Teach me to be more merciful. I humbly ask this in your holy name. Amen.

Thursday

"...But nothing unclean will enter [the New Jerusalem], nor any[one] who does abominable things or tells lies. Only those will enter whose names are written in the Lamb's book of life" (Revelation 21:27).

Be strong and courageous. Do not be afraid of anything or anyone, because God is with you. He will not forsake you. Perhaps you would rather plan the weekend activities than think about the hours you will spend in the library. Are you ever tempted to cut corners with your many obligations? Do you have lengthy papers or important projects due? What assignments are burdensome to you? While you work on them, remember that honesty and morality will lead you to heaven. Prayers will keep you in God's good graces. Where is the best place for you to pray? The Lord is kind and merciful. Why not do everything imaginable to ensure eternity with God in heaven? How can you promote honest behaviors on campus today?

Dear God,

Help me to be a virtuous student when negative forces tug at me. Keep me strong and focused on pleasing you. I only desire you. You are my light and salvation. Amen.

Friday/Saturday

"Long-suffering results in great wisdom;
   a short temper raises folly high" (Proverbs 14:29).

Control your rage. When you are stressed or upset, go for a walk or exercise the annoyance away. Ask God to bless you and fill you with his grace and wisdom to resolve the issue peacefully. Talk to God; request noble ideas and thoughts that can enable you to calmly make sense of your situation in a reasonable manner. Pray for enlightenment. Allow God to work through you in a constructive way that is both amicable and agreeable to everyone in your life. If a classmate is not at her best, embrace and love her anyway. Smile as if you were beaming into God's eyes. Maybe that person was having a terrible day and needs a friendly face and a warm smile. This small step is the first step to acting more Christ-like.

Dear God,

Teach me how to be slow to anger. Teach me to look for you in other people. Perhaps then I will speak and act even more nicely to them. I want to be like you in thoughts, words, and actions. Amen.

Thanksgiving

Sunday

"Blessed are the peacemakers,
   for they will be called children of God" (Matthew 5:9).

A peaceful environment fosters love, harmony, and order. How are you getting along with your roommate? It can be challenging to live with another person. Did you have preconceived ideas about what it would be like to have a roomie? Can you create a living space that offers tranquility and tolerance? It is not easy cultivating peacefulness among a group full of diverse thinkers and believers, but that is exactly what God wants you to do. Are you open-minded? In what ways can you work toward achieving peace at your school? What clubs or organizations promote peacefulness? Aspire to manage, work, and live productively for peace and justice. How can you do that in the classroom and dormitory today?

Dear God,

Fill me with the love that I need to live peacefully with my roommate. Give me the stamina to work placidly with students who have different values and beliefs. Thank you, dear Lord, for letting peace begin with me. Amen.

Monday

"Be angry but do not sin; do not let the sun set on your anger" (Ephesians 4:26).

Reach out to God. When you are annoyed about a situation, sort through your ambivalent feelings. Perhaps your professor has bombarded you with projects and assignments. Maybe your laptop crashed, losing your unsaved work. Perhaps someone stole your clothes from the laundry room. Whatever the circumstances are for your frustration, ask God how to quell the bitterness and replace it with love. Reflect on times when something infuriated you. Was anything positive derived from that situation? What enabled you to become amicable again? How did God work through you? What can you do in the future to promote more love, harmony, and happiness?

Dear God,

Grant me peacefulness to wash away any anger that I have been harboring. Cleanse my aching heart and soothe the hurt that has been hidden in me. Replace it with your love. Help me to be more Christ-like in all I say, think, and do. I ask this in your sweet and holy name, Lord. Amen.

Tuesday

"Offer praise as your sacrifice to God;
    fulfill your vows to the Most High" (Psalm 50:14).

Thank the Lord. Have you ever received an "award" for patronizing your favorite store? Many retailers offer additional discounts or provide cash back to their loyal customers. Airlines offer frequent-flier points to earn free tickets. It is their way of saying thanks for using their company. What could you do to thank God for all he has done for you? Think of the blessings God has showered you with. What nice gesture could you make to thank God? Try complimenting the janitor or a food-service worker at school. Identify someone you normally would not speak to and offer a kind word. That would be pleasing to God and the stranger.

Dear God,

Teach me to be more thankful to you who gives me everything. Help me to do more than simply saying "thank you." Remind me to be more appreciative through gentle nudges. You shower me with countless blessings each day. I am extremely grateful for the endless stream of glory that you fill me with. Show me how to offer you a sacrifice of thanksgiving. My mind and heart are open to you, dear Lord. Amen.

Wednesday

"And whatever you do, in word or in deed, do everything in
the name of the Lord Jesus, giving thanks to God the Father
through him" (Colossians 3:17).

Be thankful for everything. It is OK to offer the struggles of your
day to God. Perhaps you have a difficult class, a cranky professor, or
dreadful assignments. Can you give it all to God? Then your suffering
will not be in vain. Give thanks to God for everything, even if you
do not understand or are struggling with difficult moments in your
life. God does not expect you to understand at all times, but to trust.
However, God does desire you to be thankful for your life; to have an
attitude of gratitude. This means thanking God for the blessings in
your life: family, friendships, being able-bodied, intelligence, opportunities, etc. It might also mean changing your attitude toward the
challenging class, the professor who makes you cringe, and the awful
homework. What are you thankful for and how will you give thanks
for it? As you prepare your heart for Advent and during this season
of thanksgiving, you might make a concrete list of the blessings God
has given you.

Dear God,

As I busy myself with work, I offer it to you, dear Lord,
and I am thankful for everything that you have given to me.
I know there is a purpose for it all. Amen.

Thursday

"Not that I say this because of need, for I have learned, in
whatever situation I find myself, to be self-sufficient. I know
indeed how to live in humble circumstances; I know also
how to live with abundance. In every circumstance and in
all things I have learned the secret of being well fed and of
going hungry, of living in abundance and of being in need"
(Philippians 4:11–12).

Be content. Is it easy to compare yourself to the guy living down the hall or the student next to you in class? Everything could feel right in your world until you compare. Focus strictly on yourself and ask if you are content with what you have without any "if only I had this…" statements. People who seem to have it all are sometimes more discontent because one more thing eludes their grasp. Instead of wanting more, can you look inward and be thankful for all you have?

Dear God,

Help me to feel satisfied with all the blessings that you have given me. I am truly appreciative of everything that you do for me. Thank you, Lord, for the wonderful instructors and friends that you have brought into my life. You are a generous God. Amen.

Friday/Saturday

"I know your works (behold, I have left an open door before you, which no one can close). You have limited strength, and yet you have kept my word and have not denied my name" (Revelation 3:8).

God grants opportunities. When God opens a door for you, can you walk through it? God gave you all of the tools, skills, and abilities you will need to do the job he has in store for you and wants you to take advantage of the opportunities he has placed before you. To get an experience you never have had before, you must do something new. Be open-minded. Whenever you learn about an interesting prospect, remember that God set it before you. What opportunity has God led you to recently? This might be a good opportunity to evaluate how you will spend your Christmas and spring break.

Dear God,

Thank you for continuing to bring wonderful opportunities to me. Thank you for believing that I am capable and deserving. I am so fortunate to have you with me, guiding me, protecting me, and opening the world of possibilities for me to explore. I love you, Lord. Amen.

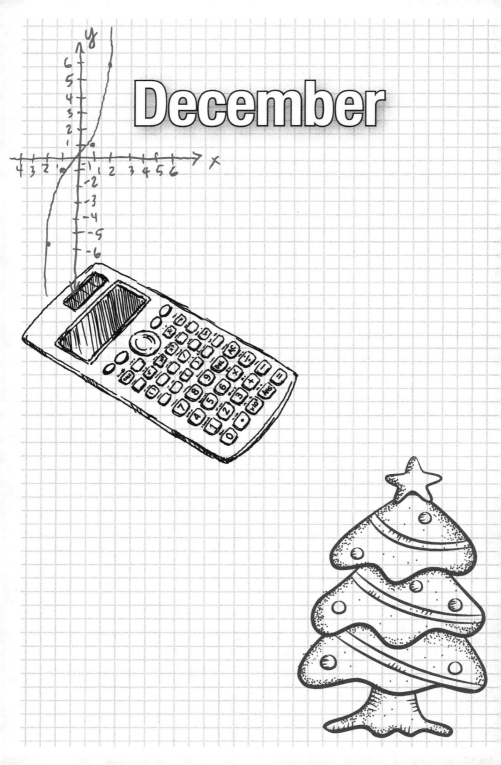

December

Holding On

Sunday

"For in hope we were saved. Now hope that sees for itself is
not hope. For who hopes for what one sees?" (Romans 8:24).

Always be hopeful. Hope is a word college students are well-acquainted
with. You hope to understand. You hope to learn and do well on your
final exams. You hope to graduate, get a job, and be successful. What
are you hopeful for? Advent is the season of joyful hope. This Advent,
ask God to help you with perseverance and enlightenment. Also, ask
the Lord for guidance during moments of failure, because tucked
inside of each failure is success waiting to emerge.

Dear God,

Give me the strength and determination to forge onward
with my studies. I like the curriculum that I have chosen,
despite its challenges. Help my mind to absorb the course
material and retain it. I believe I am at this university because
you led me here. Continue to guide me, Lord, and keep me
strong so that I can do your work and please you all of the
days of my life. I am here to serve and honor you. Amen.

Monday

"For the LORD gives wisdom, from his mouth come
knowledge and understanding" (Proverbs 2:6).

Open your Bible. What do you dream of becoming and how will you make it happen? In college you seek wisdom and pay high rates for your tuition. Are you a conscientious student with clear goals? Now your immediate attention is revolving around final exams, and thus your primary motivation is to do well on them. Widen your focus to include God in the equation. If you want meaningful wisdom, open your Bible and study it the way you would with any of your classes. God will fill your head and heart with the wisdom you need to continue your passage through school and your journey through life. Trust in God. He will make your dreams come true according to his will.

Dear God,

Do not let me get so narrowly focused on only my class work and exam preparation that I forget about you. Help me to find the time to pray. I welcome you into my life today, tomorrow, and always. Without you, my education and work lack meaning, for you pave the path to true wisdom and knowledge. Everything includes you. All I do is for you, dear Lord. Amen.

Tuesday

"Let us hold unwaveringly to our confession that gives
us hope, for he who made the promise is trustworthy"
(Hebrews 10:23).

Trust God, who keeps his promises. Do you trust your friends? Do they keep their promises? Do you keep in touch with your friends from home, or have you made several new friends who are dependable and cool to hang out with? When you trust your friends, it is because you really know them. Think about the people in your life whom you trust. God brought these extraordinary people into your life for a special reason. Perhaps they will enable you to hold firmly to hope and trust in the Lord. Get to know God so you can trust him with all of your heart and soul. Friends may break their promises and let you down, but God never will.

Dear God,

Teach me to be more trusting and depend on you more. I want your name in my mind so that I always will think of you. I want you in my heart and on my lips so that I will love you more and only have kind things to say. Amen.

Wednesday

"You have no idea what your life will be like tomorrow. You are a puff of smoke that appears briefly and then disappears" (James 4:14).

Focus on today. You do not know what tomorrow will bring. Your life is in God's hands, who is in control. Do not squander today worrying about tomorrow. What good deeds have you done today? What have you done to please God? Think about your actions this week. An introspection of your activities can get you back on track to living for today. God gave you the entire day as a gift and wants you to live it to the fullest. How can you make the most of this day? What can you do to make it the best day for you and for God?

Dear God,

Don't let me squander this day worrying about tomorrow; those concerns may never happen. Let me do incredible acts to please you today. I will not be at this university very long, however, my endeavors can make a difference and change this world, always impacting it. Thank you, Lord, for giving me this day. Amen.

Thursday

"I kneel before the Father...that he may grant you in accord with the riches of his glory to be strengthened with power through his Spirit in the inner self" (Ephesians 3:14, 16).

Allow the Holy Spirit to empower you. Give control of your life to the Holy Spirit and be amazed at the capabilities and momentum that will be released to you. The Holy Spirit will give you the strength to resist temptation as you approach the weekend, and have to decide between partying and preparing for final's week. The Holy Spirit will grant you infinite wisdom and unlimited energies to study longer and harder than you imagined possible. The Spirit will fill you with tolerance to do everything the Lord asks of you. What do you think will be an impossible feat for you today and this weekend? How will you allow the Holy Spirit to assist you as you accomplish your goals?

Dear God,

Remind me that with the Holy Spirit, I can do more than I knew possible. With you, Lord, I can do anything, if it is your will. Fill me with your living water. I love you, Lord. Amen.

Friday/Saturday

"Blessed is the man who does not walk in the counsel of the wicked, nor stand in the way of sinners, nor sit in company with scoffers. Rather, the law of the LORD is his joy; and on his law he meditates day and night" (Psalm 1:1–2)

Delight in the Lord. Every good thing is from the Lord, who grants countless blessings each day to those who follow his word. God wants you to be a kind and generous person, truthful, and loving. What can you do this weekend to be productive and respectable? Will you put a hefty emphasis on preparing for finals? When others notice what you are doing, they may be drawn to your way of living and be eager to emulate your behavior. God wants you to hang with the right crowd and set good examples for others to follow. Are you called this weekend to be a good leader while acting Christ-like?

Dear God,

Help me to start the weekend on a positive note. Bring kind and trusting people into my life so that I can study with them and prepare for final exams and finish projects. Amen.

Introspection

Sunday

"...But following exactly the way that the Lord, your God,
commanded you that you may live and prosper, and
may have long life in the land which you are to possess"
(Deuteronomy 5:33).

Let God guide you. God knows that life as a college student has peaks
and valleys. There are many demands placed on you by professors, your
parents, and even yourself. Do you feel pressure? What burdens do
you carry? Ask God to keep you focused. What obstacles are cluttering
your path: playing video games, shopping online, spending hours on
social networking Internet sites, attending sports events, hanging out
with friends in the lounge? Obey God's laws and everything will go
well for you. Do your friends struggle to obey God's laws? Remember
that God is walking your journey with you. What problems will you
give to God today?

Dear God,

Teach me to walk around the distracting and disruptive
obstacles that surround me. There are so many different
avenues I could take; some lead away from you. Do not
let me drift from you, dear Lord. Always keep me near.
You are the light of my life. Amen.

Monday

"Thus says the LORD: Stand by the earliest roads, ask the
pathways of old, 'Which is the way to good?' and walk it;
thus you will find rest for yourselves. But they said,
'We will not walk it'" (Jeremiah 6:16).

Walk the path of virtue. While your journey can be wearisome, God wants you to revitalize your spirit and enjoy the many blessings he has granted you. Pause to reflect on recent gifts you have received from God. Focus on the many wonderful aspects of your college life: the ability to make decisions about your future and perhaps modify your major, the new classes you can take next semester, the possibility of a minor in a subject you enjoy, options for participating in new recreational activities. Whatever you decide, whichever path you choose to walk, include the Lord and you will have peace.

Dear God,

Bless the choices I make today. Let them be wise and meaningful. Continue to guide me down the path of righteousness so that everything I say and do is pleasing to you. Expose me to the opportunities that you want me to embrace. Everything I do is for you, Lord. The only way to heaven is through you. Amen.

Tuesday

"Maintain good conduct among the Gentiles, so that if they speak of you as evildoers, they may observe your good works and glorify God on the day of visitation" (1 Peter 2:12).

Always maintain the highest moral character possible. Live properly among your unbelieving neighbors. Then, if they accuse you of doing wrong, they will see your honorable behavior. Are you surrounded by classmates who do not believe in God? Maybe students are Buddhists, Muslims, or atheists. Perhaps they were raised with differing standards and morals. God wants you to maintain your religious persona through modesty. Do not give anyone a reason to doubt your motives through your actions or appearance. How can you give people a reason to want to know about all of the blessings God has bestowed on you? Do you feel comfortable talking about the wonders of God with your classmates? How will you set a good example for your neighbors today?

Dear God,

Thank you for your constant blessings and infinite love.
You fill me up with grace and loveliness to share with everyone
I meet. With you, everything is good in my world. Amen.

Wednesday

"Then he said to me: 'This is the word of the LORD to
Zerubbabel: Not by might, and not by power, but by
my spirit, says the Lord of hosts" (Zechariah 4:6).

Ask the Holy Spirit to release his power within you. The Holy
Spirit dwells inside of you because you believe. The Spirit will give
you the wisdom you need in all circumstances. Ask the Holy Spirit for
guidance with your assignments. God put special people into your life
to help you: friends, campus ministers, professors, tutors, advisors, and
family members. God empowers them to connect with you through
their talents. It is through the Holy Spirit that you will be given the
power you need to do whatever God asks of you. Are you stressed?
Do you feel comfortable reaching out in your time of need? The Holy
Spirit is a merely a whisper away.

Dear God,

Release the powers of the Holy Spirit within me today as I
prepare for class. Give me the fortitude I need to understand
and apply everything that I have learned. Thank you
for always being with me as I study, learn, and live.
I am comforted by your presence in my life. Amen.

Thursday

"For he commands his angels with regard to you,
to guard you wherever you go. With their hands they shall
support you, lest you strike your foot against a stone"
(Psalm 91:11–12).

Angels surround you. God's angelic messengers are near you
throughout each day. They arrive in a stranger's smile, accolades from
a teacher, or in the helpfulness of a classmate. God also assigns all his

beloved people, namely all of humanity, with a guardian angel. Have you seen an angel? Reflect on God's goodness this week. Did something wonderful happen? Perhaps it was a compliment from a friend. When the dining hall workers speak nicely, do you recognize God's voice in them? God sends messages to remind you that he is watching over you, protecting, and showering you with his endless stream of mercy and love. As you walk to class today, notice the love that follows you—it is a gift from God.

Dear God,

Thank you, for the angels you send to safeguard me. Thank you for filling me with happiness and love; I realize these are gifts from you. Thank you for reaching out to me in such nice ways. Your love sustains me. You are the way to eternal life in heaven. Amen.

Friday/Saturday

"Therefore, sin must not reign over your mortal bodies
so that you obey their desires" (Romans 6:12).

God is powerful. Who tells you when you should go to bed? You could stay up all night. Perhaps some of your friends stay up late and sleep the next day away. Regardless of what the temptation is, stay strong. Call upon God to help you overcome the enticements. How do you prevent sin from controlling you? Saint Faustina was tricked by the devil to burn her diary describing her visions and conversations with Jesus. When this Polish nun was asked to rewrite it, she wrote more than 700 pages superbly, spreading the message of divine mercy. Several convents refused Saint Faustina because they didn't want to accept an impoverished farm maiden with little education. How can you give yourself completely to God and allow him to work through you to do what is good and right?

Dear God,

I trust in your awesome powers. Help me to do everything in moderation so that I don't become addicted to anything except loving and praising you. I ask this in your sweet and holy name. I love you, Lord. Amen.

Final Exams

Sunday

"So we are ambassadors for Christ, as if God were
appealing through us. We implore you on behalf of Christ,
be reconciled to God" (2 Corinthians 5:20).

Resign yourself to God. You may not feel like you are accomplishing much today, but by giving yourself to God, you are letting him know you are ready, willing, and able to do whatever it is he calls you to do. Perhaps you are already doing it without even realizing it. God is mysterious and you do not have to concern yourself about understanding the will of God. You are pleasing God through prayer and your daily grind. Tests are essential in college; but they are difficult to prepare for and take. If you have resigned yourself to God, he will work with you, through you, and in you.

Dear God,

Help me to regurgitate everything that I learned so I do well on my exams. Help me to retain this information to apply it in my future field of study. Everything I have learned thus far will be reflected in my impending career. Thank you for bringing me to this place in my life to prepare me to ultimately do your work. Amen.

Monday

> "There are many parts, yet one body. The eye cannot say
> to the hand, 'I do not need you,' nor again the head to the
> feet, 'I do not need you.' Now you are Christ's body, and
> individually parts of it" (1 Corinthians 12:20–21, 27).

God has a purpose for you. You may not fully comprehend what it is, but there is a distinctive place for you. Do you ever feel as if you do not belong? God wants all that you do to have meaning. Can you put your faith in God today as you take exams and submit projects? In time you will understand where you are meant to be and what you are supposed to do. College tests are steppingstones to a richer knowledge base. Today, have the courage to step out on that path by taking your final exams. God is with you in the examination room.

> Dear God,
>
> I trust you with my heart and soul. Be with me as I embark on my finals. Help me to do well so that I can take the next step toward doing your work. I ask this in your sweet name, Lord Jesus. Amen.

Tuesday

> "Desire without knowledge is not good;
> and whoever acts hastily, blunders" (Proverbs 19:2).

Be still. With so many obligations you might rush through projects and work halfheartedly and inevitably overlook something important, or make mistakes. Do not overcommit and spread yourself too thin. Instead, focus on what you can and must do. On the feast of the Immaculate Conception, reflect on Mary's conception without original sin and how she obeyed God even though Adam and Eve did not. Pray to Mary, full of grace, to watch over you. Take a moment to be silent and reflect on God's love for you and Mary's devotion to serve God. What are some of your academic and spiritual achievements this semester? How has your devotedness developed at school? During these weeks of final exams, take time to study, prepare, and pray.

Dear God,

Cast my anxieties away as I prepare for final exams.
Extinguish my fear of failure and replace it with love for you.
Expand my mind so that I can hold the knowledge I have
acquired and use it accordingly. I adore you, my sweet,
loving Lord. Amen.

Wednesday

"Beloved, do not be surprised that a trial by fire is occurring
among you, as if something strange were happening to you.
But rejoice to the extent that you share in the sufferings
of Christ, so that when his glory is revealed you may also
rejoice exultantly" (1 Peter 4:12–13).

Offer up your anguish to Jesus. Suffering helps you to understand
the torture Jesus endured on the cross. He suffered and died to grant
you eternal life in heaven. Ask God to enlighten you as you work
through your tests. Exams are looming overhead like a big dark cloud,
but today imagine the bright sunshine behind them. Hidden in you is
a bright sun too—the Holy Spirit. Do you believe the Holy Spirit will
keep you strong? Ask God to take the exam with you. Call upon your
guardian angel, too. You have an amazing celestial force protecting you.

Dear God,

Thank you for surrounding me with a ring of holiness
to diminish my anxiety and keep me strong for my
examinations. Your love lifts me up. Amen.

Thursday

"My soul, be at rest in God alone, from whom comes my
hope. God alone is my rock and my salvation, my fortress;
I shall not fall. My deliverance and honor are with God,
my strong rock; my refuge is with God" (Psalm 62:6–8).

God will always safeguard you. As you begin this day, no matter what battle you face, remember not to be shaken, because God is your rock and salvation. Reflect on your commitment during the school year to stay on the right path, study hard, and make time for others. Reflect on your devotion to your spirituality this semester. Have you been drawn closer to God? If so, in what way? Continue to rely on the Lord and Savior. He will protect, defend, and save you. Do you have the courage to put all of your faith in God to help you through your exams? How will you do that? What can you do today to show God how much you love him?

Dear God,

Stay with me as I take my last round of exams. Hold me up and pour your love over me to rejuvenate me. I need you. Amen.

Friday/Saturday

"The human heart plans the way,
but the LORD directs the steps" (Proverbs 16:9).

Make a plan and let God guide you. Without plans you will wander aimlessly. It is wise to have a strategy for your future and set realistic goals. It is sensible to outline next semester's courses, plan a curriculum, and shoot for the moon. You might not make it there, but if you land on a star, that would be good, too! Allow God into your life to help plot your course according to his plans. With the Lord at the helm, you will surely make it past the stars and into heaven. As you leave school on break, what plans will you make to occupy your vacation time? How will you transition back into your family life at home?

Dear God,

Thank you for enabling me to get through the grueling week of final exams and for completing all of my projects this semester at school. Keep me safe as I travel home for the holidays. Thank you for the gift of family and friends. I am thankful for the countless blessings you have given me. I truly love you, Lord. Amen.

Christmas Break

Sunday

"Willingly serve the Lord and not human beings, knowing that each will be requited from the Lord for whatever good he does, whether he is slave or free" (Ephesians 6:7–8).

Provide service with a smile. Remember, whatever good you do, you will receive the same from the Lord. Your love is reflected to God in the compassion and attentiveness in which you serve others. This is not always easy to do, especially if you are tired or overwhelmed. God wants genuine joy and if you can muster up the fortitude to give it, you will be blessed. What tasks will you do today that will require an effort to be jolly? What service projects will you do in anticipation of the Christmas celebration? Remember that it is in giving that you receive.

Dear God,

Let me be joyous while I do chores and help with holiday preparations. Assist me in providing service to others in my community. Open my eyes so that I can see the good in others. Fill my heart with the love and warmth that I know you want me to feel and share this season. Amen.

Monday

"My strength, for you I watch; you, God, are my fortress" (Psalm 59:10).

Waiting is never easy. Think about every time you waited in a doctor's office. You probably thought a lot while you waited. Perhaps you silently rehearsed questions with built-up anticipation. That is what God wants you to do while you wait for him. God has a purpose for everything, and the Lord's timing is perfect. Can you let God be your strength and your fortress? During the last week of Advent, what can you do to make waiting for Christmas truly meaningful? How can you procure and contain your escalating excitement for Christmas in a dynamic way to benefit others?

> Dear God,
>
> I have confidence in your strength. You are my refuge, dear Lord. Bless my waiting, making it productive and significant so that I might touch the hearts of others. Allow me to focus on others and not on my own self-gain. Teach me how to be patient and loving while I wait for you. Shine through me and let me be a true example of your goodness to everyone I meet. Amen.

Tuesday

> "Do not store up for yourselves treasures on earth, where moth and decay destroy, and thieves break in and steal. But store up treasures in heaven, where neither moth nor decay destroys, nor thieves break in and steal. For where your treasure is, there also will your heart be" (Matthew 6:19–21).

Bring memories and love to heaven. Do not get caught up in worldly possessions because they will weigh you down and cause greediness. Instead, be generous with what you have. Treasures on earth are temporary and cannot be taken into heaven. Invest in love and kindness so that you can enjoy God's eternal rewards forever. When you go to heaven, you can bring memories of the good deeds you did on earth. What memories will you take with you? What are some activities you can do in your community or church during your break from school?

Dear God,

Guide me to the organizations that need me. Work through me to do wondrous deeds for those around me. I ask this in your sweet name, Lord. Amen.

Wednesday

"We know that all things work for good for those who love God, who are called according to his purpose" (Romans 8:28).

Good things happen to those who love God. You might not see it, feel it, or believe it today, or this year, but God weaves all of the events of your life together for your good. The summation of your past events come together as a whole throughout your life. The events you attended this last semester combined with good or poor test grades; and the club meetings mixed with late nights at the library. Compare your life converging the way Christmas cookies are made. Each ingredient gets tossed into a bowl. Each item is ordinary and does not taste good alone. When it is stirred and baked, it is wonderfully delicious. Last semester's classes, socials, and exams might have seemed trivial in the scheme of things, but God will intertwine it all so that eventually, as a whole, your life will be good.

Dear God,

Thank you for all you have given to me, the good and the bad. I trust and love you completely. Amen.

Thursday

"Rejoice in hope, endure in affliction, persevere in prayer" (Romans 12:12).

Rejoice in hope while being patient. Waiting can be agonizing. Not only are you waiting for Christmas to arrive, but you must wait for your grades to be posted and next semester to begin. Be patient and prayerful. Keeping optimistic is the first step on the path to success with God leading the way. Put your heart into Christmas preparations.

Reflect on all that God has done for you this year. How can you thank
him for it? Give yourself time for spiritual reflection and ask God to
continue to help you as Advent draws to a close.

Dear God,

You have given so much to me throughout this past year, and
I am truly grateful. Each time I show you my empty hands,
you fill them with more blessings than I can hold. Teach me
how to share those bountiful gifts with others. Enable me to
take some time to give to others and help me to see those in
need around me. Let me be an extension of your goodness.
Amen.

Friday/Saturday

"Then the LORD answered me and said: Write down the vision;
make it plain upon tablets, so that the one who reads it may run.
For the vision is a witness for the appointed time, a testimony
to the end; it will not disappoint. If it delays, wait for it, it will
surely come, it will not be late" (Habakkuk 2:2–3).

Patience is a virtue. When you were a child, wasn't it unbearable
waiting for Santa to arrive? That is how God wants you to wait for him.
Have you ever tried to manipulate God, telling him that you are doing his will while having a hidden agenda? You cannot fool God, only
yourself. Saint Gianna Beretta Molla wanted to be a missionary, but
when it did not happen, she prayed while she waited. It was through
patience that she discovered God chose an entirely different profession
for her. She learned that following God's will can be a slow process.
How can you develop patience while you wait for God to reveal his
plan for your life and career path?

Dear God,

Help me to have the patience of Saint Gianna
while I wait for you. Amen.

Christmas

Sunday

"They were overjoyed at seeing the star" (Matthew 2:10).

Ask for a sign. What if God gave you a sign as ordinary as a star in the sky? Would you follow it? Tonight, gaze upon the stars that dot the sky and imagine what it was like for the wise men to follow one. Their patience on such a long journey is commendable, for they were uncertain about what they would find. Learn from their hopefulness as you continue with your own journey through life. You really do not know what you will find. When God gives you a sign, like the star that the wise men followed, do not second-guess it. Anticipate with the same exuberance that the wise men felt so many years ago. When Saint John Chrysostom asked God for a sign to ensure that he was interpreting Scriptures correctly, God gave him one. Has God given you a sign, but you did not recognize it as one? What can you do to increase your awareness of signs that God has given you?

Dear God,

Help me to see you in everything:
the gifts, the blessings, and the signs. Amen.

Monday

"[Mary] gave birth to her firstborn son. She wrapped him in swaddling clothes and laid him in a manger, because there was no room for them in the inn" (Luke 2:7).

Think of Mary. Throughout your life you will encounter times when there may not be room for you in a program, class, or activity. Act as Mary did and make do with what you have. Mary made the best of her situation and did so with grace and much love. Have there been times last semester where you had to make the best of an awkward or uncomfortable situation? Mary must have been frightened without her mother's advice and guidance. She put her complete trust and faith in God that he would provide. Reflect on the times where you put your faith in God. How did that work out? When God asks something of you, will you respond as Mary did and comply wholeheartedly?

Dear God,

During this holy Christmas season, remind me of the devotion of Joseph and Mary to obey you unequivocally. Teach me to open my heart to you as Mary did, and help me to think of Mary during my trials and tribulations. Amen.

Tuesday

"So they went in haste and found Mary and Joseph, and the infant lying in the manger"(Luke 2:16).

Jesus was not born in a palace. There were no silks or fine linens to swaddle him. He came into the world in an earthen manager, surrounded by animals and slept in a food trough. He was like the hope diamond on a sandy beach. You expect to find shells, not a jewel. Yet the shepherds found their Lord in an unusual place *a crèche.* This humbling route enabled him to relate to the poor, working class, and all people everywhere. Isn't it amazing that the Savior of the world picked this place? Have you ever considered how you will enter the workforce? Will it be in a humbling manner or with royal panache? What will you do to humble yourself over your Christmas holiday?

Dear God,

Thank you for giving your only begotten Son for me. You said whoever believes in him will have eternal life. I will show you my thanks by offering gifts of charity while I am on my school break, thus giving to others the way you gave to me. Amen.

Wednesday

> "And having been warned by God in a dream not to return
> to Herod, [the magi] departed for their own country by
> another way" (Matthew 2:12).

Pray through Mary's intercession. During the Christmas season
and especially on the feast of the Solemnity of Mary, think of the role
she played in your salvation. Recall Mary's fortitude as she brought
Jesus into the world. Her arduous journey into Bethlehem was over
eighty miles long, and she was not wearing tennis shoes. The terrain
was harsh, yet she never complained. When she camped out overnight,
she didn't have gear from name-brand stores. She slept on the cold,
hard ground. After giving birth, she traveled nearly 250 miles with
a newborn baby, as God instructed her, trusting the Lord implicitly.
Has God called you to do something extraordinary? Perhaps you were
asked to provide food or companionship to someone you are not fond
of from your church or family. Pray to Mary for strength and courage when God calls on you. When he does, what will you say and do?

Dear God,

Teach me to be charitable and give to others.
Remind me to turn to Mary for inspiration. Amen.

Thursday

> "[This woman] was completely occupied with good deeds
> and almsgiving" (Acts 9:36).

Let Jesus work through you. God calls you to do good deeds and
help the less fortunate. You don't have to take a mission trip volunteering in an impoverished country on your school break. But God wants
you to be mindful to give to the less fortunate. Think for a moment
about something you can do right now that would please God. Could
you do something simple; talk to someone you otherwise would not
notice? Maybe you could compliment a stranger or volunteer to teach
someone to read. Could you start out small and each week increase
your level of giving? Saint Nicholas gave gifts to needy families, leaving
them secretly on doorsteps. Could you be like Saint Nicholas? Open
your heart and let God work within you.

Dear God,

Help me to do your work today, whatever it is. Help me to be open to it, to understand it, and give me the courage and strength to complete it. I am here to do your work, Lord. Work through me. I am ready, willing, and able. Amen.

Friday/Saturday

"Our steps are from the LORD;
how, then, can mortals understand their way?"
(Proverbs 20:24).

God is in control of your life. As the feast of the Epiphany approaches, celebrate that God revealed Jesus' true identity as the Savior of the World. How will this impact your decisions for the new year? Just as you would arrange to reconnect with friends over your school break, it is also sensible to talk to God. Use prayer to strengthen your bond with the Lord. Ask God to bless your plans and guide your steps as you embark on another new semester at school. Do not waste your time or energy trying to sift through chaos to make sense of it all. Give it to God, for he knows what he is doing. There is a reason for everything that happens. Nothing is random. When you are bewildered while making your plans, turn to God and recall the feast of the Epiphany. How will you include God in your strategies next semester? What are your goals both academically and spiritually? How will you draw God nearer next year?

Dear God,

Thank you for a productive year of growth and opportunity. Amen.

Don't Quit!

When things go wrong, as they sometimes will;
* when the road you're trudging seems all uphill,*

When the funds are low and the debts are high,
* and you want to smile, but you have to sigh,*

When care is pressing you down a bit,
* rest, if you must, but don't you quit.*

Life is queer with its twists and turns,
* as every one of us sometimes learns,*

And many a failure turns about,
* when he might have won had he stuck it out;*

Don't give up though the pace seems slow—
* You may succeed with another blow.*

Often the goal is nearer than
* it seems to a faint and faltering man,*

Often the struggler has given up,
* when he might have captured the victor's cup,*

And he learned too late when the night slipped down,
* how close he was to the golden crown.*

Success is failure turned inside out—
* the silver tint of the clouds of doubt,*

And you never can tell how close you are;
* it may be near when it seems so far,*

So stick to the fight when you're hardest hit—
* It's when things seem worst that you must not quit.*

Author unknown

January

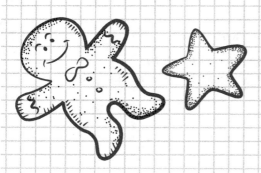

Another Fresh Start

Sunday

"This is the day the LORD has made;
let us rejoice in it and be glad" (Psalm 118:24).

Let God guide your journey. Every year you are given the opportunity to wipe the slate clean and start over. God gives you another chance for improvement. What can you do to make this semester even better than the last one? There are so many possibilities for you in the future. Have you wondered about them? Rejoice and be glad in all that you can do with God's love. This is an exciting time, living in the academic arena knowing God has given you so much. All you have to do is accept his will and take the first step forward. This day is God's gift to you, and what you do with it is your gift to the Lord.

Dear God,

Fill me with the courage I need to make a fresh start. Enable me to make wise choices throughout my school year. Fill me with your love and joy, kind and merciful, Lord, and remind me that you are always with me and that I have nothing to fear. Amen.

Monday

"I have the strength for everything through him
who empowers me" (Philippians 4:13).

God empowers. When you feel vulnerable or unsure of what you are capable of doing, ask God to empower you. Mountains can be moved, raging fires can be extinguished, stormy seas calmed, if it is God's will. Reflect on the mountains in your life that God has moved for you. What were they? Did God help you through a difficulty last semester? No task is too great for your Lord and Savior. Call upon him for help. He can provide the stamina you need to continue onward. Put your faith in God, and he will enable you to persevere. God will help you on every step of the way through school. As you order your textbooks, how will you rekindle the strength of the Holy Spirit inside of you?

Dear God,

Strengthen me today so I can accomplish the tasks I face. When I feel overwhelmed with all I must do in planning my career path, help me to be energized with the powers of the Holy Spirit so that I can jump over the many hurdles in front of me. Amen.

Tuesday

"This momentary light affliction is producing for us
an eternal weight of glory beyond all comparison"
(2 Corinthians 4:17).

Let God carry your burdens. Get to know the campus faculty because they can help you solve many of your logistical problems. Through conversations with them, you might begin to realize what your true interests are. Those discussions could be jumping-off points to emerging future passions. Your troubles might be small to them. Difficulties make you stronger and develop your character, so thank God for them. Something good will come from every difficulty if you look for it. Saint Teresa of Ávila overcame numerous dilemmas and hardships and founded the convent of Carmelite Nuns. For nearly two years she had visions of Jesus. She spent hours in mental prayer meditating on his words and face. She is the patron of headaches and body ailments. This Spanish nun gave her troubles to God. Can you? God comforts those who love him. Be amazed at what you can do with God.

Dear God,

Fill me with grace. Energize my spirit and work through me to move mountains, shape landscapes, and establish organizations beyond my capabilities. With you, anything is possible. Amen.

Wednesday

"Do not worry about tomorrow; tomorrow will take care of itself. Sufficient for a day is its own evil" (Matthew 6:34).

Worrying is counterproductive. When you worry, you can make yourself physically ill, and nothing good will come of it. Instead, can you pray and ask God to take your anxieties away? Trust that God has a plan for you. What apprehensions are you concealing that prevent you from relying on God's purpose for you? Perhaps if you encounter and work toward eliminating your fears, your worry will disappear. God knows what tomorrow will bring, and together you and God can get through anything! Can you have prayerful reflection about all of the blessings that God has given to you over the past year and thank him for them? Dwell on God's infinite love for you and rejoice in where that adoration and loyalty will take you. Contemplate ways to avoid pitfalls in the new semester. In what ways can you become a stronger individual and a better student? What changes will you make?

Dear God,

Take my worry and fears away and replace them with your infinite stream of love and joy. You are all I need. Amen.

Thursday

"I will instruct you and show you the way you should walk, give you counsel with my eye upon you" (Psalm 32:8).

Listen to God. It is not easy to have blind faith, but sometimes this is necessary when listening to God. Because the Lord loves you, he will never lead you astray. God will put the right people in your path at precisely the right time to facilitate your success. Reflect on the past where you suspected God's influence. Did you completely trust God in that situation? As you begin another semester, how will you continue to trust in God to guide you through it? God will send you messages that you will not be able to deny. How do you plan to keep your heart open to hear the Lord?

Dear God,

Help me to recognize and listen to your messages. There is so much noise and discombobulation in my life that I fear I might misinterpret your advice. Clear the clutter from my day. Quiet me and fill me with the spirit so that I will recognize, listen, and respect you when you speak. Amen.

Friday/Saturday

"But I trust in you, LORD; I say, 'You are my God.'
My destiny is in your hands; rescue me from my enemies,
from the hands of my pursuers" (Psalm 31:15–16).

God is in control of everything. When your life seems unmanageable, remember to trust in God. Give yourself completely to God, putting everything in his hands. Listen with your heart and the Lord will direct your path. Can you trust in the Lord the way Saint Augustine did? He was an excellent philosophy student, always thirsting for wisdom. However, he lost his faith and struggled with a myriad of quandaries, but God still enlightened him with wisdom and directed his steps. Augustine's faith was restored and ultimately he opened a monastery. He is known for his passionate writing, for being a brilliant teacher, and is considered a doctor of the faith. When he was a philosophy student, he had no idea what God had in store for him. Can you let God shape you?

Dear God,

Keep evil away so I can focus on pleasing you and on doing well in my studies. With you beside me, I can achieve many goals and be your humble servant. Amen.

Be True to Yourself

Sunday

> "Therefore, putting away falsehood, speak the truth,
> each one to his neighbor, for we are members one of
> another" (Ephesians 4:25).

Speak the truth. If a friend or roommate asks a question that you are afraid to answer, will you have the courage to be honest? One little white lie might seem harmless, but it creates room to spin a web of deceit, confusion, and destruction, possibly taking you to a place you had no intention of going. Instead, speak softly and from the heart. Often it is not what you say, but how you say it. Think back to a time when you were sorry you grappled with truthfulness last semester. Today, ask the Holy Spirit to help you find the right words to deliver all of your messages with honesty and integrity.

> Dear God,
> Form the perfect words in my mind so that I always speak
> the truth in love. Put the right words in my mouth so that
> I can lovingly express what I carry in my heart. Help me to
> be honest and tender so my best intentions shine with your
> guidance. Amen.

Monday

> "How many are my foes, LORD! How many rise against me!
> How many say of me, 'There is no salvation for him in God.'
> But you, LORD, are a shield around me; my glory, you keep
> my head high" (Psalm 3:2–4).

Don't compromise your ethics. You are surrounded by a campus full of people who were raised with different beliefs. Some might have been raised with questionable morals, or perhaps no religion at all. Do you know people whose actions seem to lack virtue? Hold firmly onto your high principles and set a good example for others to emulate. Perhaps all they need is a steadfast role model. It isn't always easy to take a stand, especially if you are alone in your opinions. Remember that God is always with you to shield you against danger.

> Dear God,
>
> Lift up my head and heart to you in heaven and reign over all. Surround me with your loving arms and protect me as I align myself with you and all of the angels and saints. Fill me with your love and guide me to be a prosperous paradigm of virtue in all that I say and do. Amen.

Tuesday

> "Consider it all joy, my brothers, when you encounter various trials, for you know that the testing of your faith produces perseverance. And let perseverance be perfect, so that you may be perfect and complete, lacking in nothing" (James 1:2–4).

Tests build endurance. When troubles find you, consider it an opportunity for growth. When your faith is tested, your stamina has room to grow. Has your faith been tested at the university? What caused your trust to be questioned? How can you promote a healthy and holy endurance on campus? A pearl is created out of grit. The irritation of sand in shell causes the oyster to transform it into a precious gem. The next time you feel yourself being tested, remember the pearl. In the end, after having a chance to grow, you will be more genuine and loyal toward God and others. The challenges in life will convert you into a more beautiful, well-rounded person, who is more capable of overcoming future obstacles with grace and dignity. What challenges have you had to overcome this semester that affected your spirituality?

Dear God,

Be with me during my challenges at school.
I only want to love and serve you. Amen.

Wednesday

"Take care, then, how you hear. To anyone who has,
more will be given, and from the one who has not, even
what he seems to have will be taken away" (Luke 8:18).

Listen for God's voice. As you go to class today, enjoy the chilly temperatures and the beauty of winter. What is your favorite aspect of this season? Unplug your Mp3 Player, turn off your phone, and listen for God's voice. Be alert. Always keep your heart open so that you will not miss an opportunity to hear God, who so desires to speak to you. Pay attention to how you hear because those who listen to God will understand more fully God's mysteries. When you do this, God will shower you with abundant blessings and joy. What can you do to ensure you will hear God's voice today? Will God speak to you through another person? How will you understand his message? Whenever you struggle with interpretations, pray, read the Bible, and perform acts of service. Then, God will enlighten you.

Dear God,

Speak to me. My heart is open and I am attentive to your
voice. I am listening as I plod along on my college journey.
Amen.

Thursday

"As a father has compassion on his children, so the LORD has
compassion on those who fear him. For he knows how we
are formed, remembers that we are dust" (Psalm 103:13–14).

Humans have frailties. Just as you still need your parents, you also need God. If you stumble on your college journey, God will keep you going and enable you to recover. It's not unusual to feel lonely on campus even though you are surrounded by so many people. Do you miss your family or friends from home? Celebrate the quiet moments because it is an opportunity to invite God into your life. Has someone recently "unfriended" you through a social network? God is always present in your life and knows what is in your heart because he made it. What frailties have kept you from God? What can you do to get back into his graces? Talk to God today.

Dear God,

Help me to rise above my frailties and insecurities and reach out to you, my loving and merciful Lord. Remove the cloud of doubt that looms over me and allow me to improve physically, emotionally, and spiritually. Let me always put you first in my life. Amen.

Friday/Saturday

"So faith, hope, love remain, these three;
  but the greatest of these is love" (1 Corinthians 13:13).

The essence of God is love. Faith is a gift from God and a foundation on which we ought to build our lives. Hope helps us to remember that the good promised will indeed come to fruition, and love is the deepest reality of God inviting us to enter by sharing ourselves with others. As you review your busy schedule and plan your day, how will you enact faith, hope, and love throughout the day and weekend? Is there a professor, advisor, or lab partner that requires extra effort to be friendly? When you see this individual, can you remember that God wants you to love that person as you love him? Evoke your strong faith in God, how deeply you trust him, and how devoted you are to him.

Dear God,

Fill me with grace so I can be more loving to everyone around me. Help me to remember the people I encounter are decent people who could be burdened with a heavy load. Remind me that a kind word might make a world of difference to them. Work through me to be more loving today and every day. Amen.

Campus Community

Sunday

> "When Jesus saw this he became indignant and said to them,
> 'Let the children come to me; do not prevent them,
> for the kingdom of God belongs to such as these.
> Amen, I say to you, whoever does not accept the kingdom
> of God like a child will not enter it'" (Mark 10:14–15).

The kingdom of God belongs to children. You are in a crossover phase between leaving your childhood behind and entering adulthood. This transformation continues to change and grow immensely during this time. Does your university have an engaging and fun "bucket list" of things to do before graduation? When you participate in these experiences, can you rejoice and cherish the moments? How can you continue to grow spiritually while cherishing your childlike nature? Nourish your inner child frequently throughout your life because this will keep you youthful and grounded. Examine your own childlike qualities that enhance your personality; and name a few of your own that are beautiful and virtuous. How can you use them to enhance your faithfulness? What traits will you keep and what ones will you let go?

Dear God,

Help me to be childlike in your eyes. Let me become the person you always intended for me to be. Amen.

Monday

> "Two are better than one: They get a good wage for their toil.
> If the one falls, the other will help the fallen one. But woe to
> the solitary person! If that one should fall, there is no other
> to help" (Ecclesiastes 4:9–10).

God gave you the gift of community. Delight in your entire university experience because it is a gift. Each person has a purpose and can be a source of wealth, stimulation, and nourishment. Does your university host faith-based dinners or conferences? Have the courage to extend yourself to others on your campus by accepting an invitation to attend a community function. How can you be a source of inspiration to them and give encouragement when it is needed? Reflect on the past occasions where you have benefitted spiritually from your campus community. How can you give back to them?

Dear God,

Open my eyes to the gifts that await me on my campus. Don't let me pass them by; but instead help me realize what you want me to do. Lessen my fear as I step outside of my comfort zone and reach out to others. Fill me with your generous love. Amen.

Tuesday

"He who gets wisdom loves his own soul;
  he who keeps understanding will find good" (Proverbs 19:8).

Knowledge is a gift that you give to yourself. Learn all that you possibly can while your brain is pliable and your youthful body malleable. Consider how the phone has developed over time. By learning about it and adapting to people's needs, it has grown from a rotary phone attached to the wall, to a cordless smart phone that can talk! Phones that were once so big and clunky have been shrunk into devices that fit as an earpiece. Knowledge cannot be taken from you, and you can never get too much of it. What will you do with it? How will you use it to serve God? Will you consider acquiring more knowledge to understand God better? How will you accomplish this? The next time you use your phone to send a text, ask yourself how you will apply your knowledge for the benefit of others.

Dear God,

Guide me to do everything right and to be productive today. Help me to be conscientious in all I say, think, and do. I love you, Lord. Amen.

Wednesday

"Worry weighs down the heart, but a kind word gives it joy" (Proverbs 12:25).

Do God's work. Have you ever been in a good mood only to be brought down by somebody's negativity? Try to bring a ray of sunshine to brighten someone's day. Offer a kind word or compliment someone. Do you know someone whose spirit could use a lift? Perhaps you can identify with a frowning professor or classmate. Ask God for guidance in directing you to the right person, asking the Holy Spirit to enlighten you with the words that person needs to hear. Words cost nothing and take little effort but go a long way to making someone feel good. When you make the effort to give of yourself to someone, you are doing God's work and that is pleasing to him. How will you do God's work today?

Dear God,

Remove any angst in my heart. Replace it with love so that I can offer kindness to everyone I encounter today. I want to be a thoughtful student, offering caring and thoughtful words to those around me. I adore you, Lord. Amen.

Thursday

"Blessed be the name of God forever and ever,
    for wisdom and power are his" (Daniel 2:20).

Thank God for everything. As you would thank someone for a gift, you also need to thank God for all he gives you. Perhaps you had a "close call" last week or you avoided an accident. Thank God for that. Did you find a scholarship you can apply for? Did you make a new friend at school? Thank God for your grades, even if you were not completely satisfied with them. God freed your mind to absorb the material you studied and grants you wisdom and understanding. Thank God for everything that happens to you because he is responsible for it all. After a while, giving thanks will become second nature, and God will look favorably on you for it. What do you need to thank God for? How can you remember to thank him each time something happens to you?

Dear God,

Thank you for giving me a grateful heart. Thank you for all of the gifts you have given me this semester. Let me be mindful to thank you before I do anything else. Amen.

Friday/Saturday

"In their distress they cried to the LORD,
    who saved them in their peril;
    he brought them forth from darkness and the shadow
    of death and broke their chains asunder.
    Let them thank the LORD for his mercy, such wondrous
    deeds for the children of Adam." (Psalm 107:13–15).

God grants understanding. Have you ever stared at a book you just read and wondered what it meant? Have you ever walked out of a classroom and thought about how much you do not know and still need to learn? Have you ever been confused during a course lecture? If so, ask God to rescue you. He will bring you into the light where you will understand. God grants understanding so offer a prayer for enlightenment. Trust in God, then praise him for it. Also, reflect on what you still need to know spiritually.

Dear God,

Remove the shadows that surround me. Bathe me in your warm light and allow your love to wash me sparkling clean. Permit me to start fresh, to comprehend, and retain the knowledge I seek at my university. Thank you, Lord, for always being there for me. Amen.

Personal Growth

Sunday

"For God so loved the world that he gave his only Son,
so that everyone who believes in him might not perish
but might have eternal life" (John 3:16).

Turn to Jesus. Are you taking a particularly difficult class this semester? Perhaps the cold winter weather is bothersome. Maybe you are less enthusiastic about a club or activity you once enjoyed. Whatever is slowing you down, turn to Jesus. Let Christ be the light at the end of your tunnel. Whenever you are struggling with something, look at a crucifix and remember the pain that Jesus endured for you. Remember the sacrifice that God made by giving his only son so that you could have eternal life. Will that knowledge give you the strength necessary to forge onward? Dealing with your difficulties can make you stronger. Be like a ball of clay that is molded and then thrown into a fire. Heat makes it stronger and last longer.

Dear God,

Help me with the challenge (_____) that I am dealing with.
Help me to endure and overcome it. Be with me, Lord, so
that I can accomplish the tasks set before me at school and do
your work. Amen.

Monday

"As a mother comforts her child, so I will comfort you;
in Jerusalem you shall find your comfort" (Isaiah 66:13).

God's love for you is endless. Sometimes professors give an analogy to make a point regarding a topic that is imperative for you to know. In Isaiah, God offers an image to enable you to understand how great his love is. He compares it to the comfort and affection of a mother. God knew that you would be able to comprehend the depth of your mother's love because most of us are deeply cherished by our mothers; so this image offers us a glimpse at the Almighty's infinite love for us. Always remember when you are feeling down to call out to God, who will comfort you in a mysterious and miraculous way. What do you need comfort with today?

> Dear God,
>
> I need to feel your loving arms around me as I toil over papers and talk to my professors or classmates. Remind me that you are always there guiding and loving me. Be the beacon of hope that I long for. I am vulnerable on this campus. Comfort me, my sweet and compassionate Lord. Amen.

Tuesday

> "The LORD is good to all,
>   compassionate toward all your works" (Psalm 145:9).

Everyone makes mistakes. Blunders are a part of your humanity, which Jesus understands. Be contrite in heart and the Lord will have compassion. He made you and knows what you possess. Do you have faults that you want to give to God? Let him release you from them. Can you learn from your inadequacies? Saint Martin of Tours accepted Communion from a bishop who murdered innocent people to free innocent prisoners. He was wrought with guilt for having done so until an angel appeared and comforted him. Saint Martin is noted for performing many miracles and having visions. This Hungarian saint is the patron for alcoholics and the impoverished. Can you ask Saint Martin to intercede on your behalf? What is weighing heavy on your heart? How will you seek forgiveness and move on?

Dear God,

Have mercy on my soul. I place my contrite heart at your feet, begging for your mercy and love. Wash it clean and fill it with the joy that I long for. Amen.

Wednesday

"The LORD bless you and keep you!
The LORD let his face shine upon you,
   and be gracious to you!
The LORD look upon you kindly and give you peace!"
(Numbers 6:24–26).

God will bless you. Have Thursdays become like Fridays on your campus? Many universities host "thirsty Thursday" events, enticing students away from libraries, study groups, and lecture halls. How will you offset your assignments with downtime? Reflect on your week and tell God your disillusionments and joys, for he wants to know both. Think about your mindset for today and how you will overcome predicaments. Is anything troubling you? Ask God to shine his love on you and to help you come to terms with whatever is concerning you, whether it is concentrating on homework or untangling a miscommunication. No matter how big or small the problem is, can you give it to God? Ask him to fill you with peacefulness and wisdom to overcome the hurdles in your path. Then you can spread that serenity to everyone you encounter.

Dear God,

Thank you for always blessing me. You are one constant I can always depend on. Thank you for lifting me up. Amen.

Thursday

"The righteous cry out, the LORD hears and he rescues
   them from all their afflictions. The LORD is close to the
   brokenhearted, saves those whose spirit is crushed.
   Many are the troubles of the righteous, but the LORD
   delivers him from them all" (Psalm 34:18–20).

God rescues those in need. Have you received an unjust grade? Perhaps your computer crashed or something was lost or stolen. Maybe you are struggling with a class or a friendship. Quiet yourself and talk to Jesus, who hears the brokenhearted and saves those with crushed spirits. He will watch over you and keep you from harm. Give your brokenness to God, who will rescue you from all of your troubles. Reflect on incidents in your past when you turned to God. How did that situation resolve? What can you do to strengthen your faith? When was the last time you invited the Lord to listen to you and help you with your decisions? What is God trying to say to you?

Dear God,

Be with me. Encourage me. Strengthen me. Heal me.
Love me. Please help me, Lord, in my time of need. Amen.

Friday/Saturday

"The LORD, in whose presence I have always walked, will
send his angel with you and make your journey successful"
(Genesis 24:40).

Angels from heaven safeguard you. Are you mindful of the blue lights as you walk alone on campus at night? A guardian angel watches over you and protects you as you hurry back to your dorm. What other instances might be frightening at school? It can be intimidating to give a presentation, talk to the financial advisor, or apply for a part-time job. Perhaps you need to confront someone. Whatever stressful situation you face today, remember that your guardian angel is beside you waiting to be called upon. Not only does the Lord walk with you and the Holy Spirit dwell within you, but God has also provided you with a guardian angel!

Dear God,

Empower my guardian angel to protect me and assist me
with all I say and do today. Keep me safe and strong as I
meander about campus. I have studied and am prepared for
my classes, but still I need your help to accomplish my goals.
I ask this in your sweet and holy name, Lord. Amen.

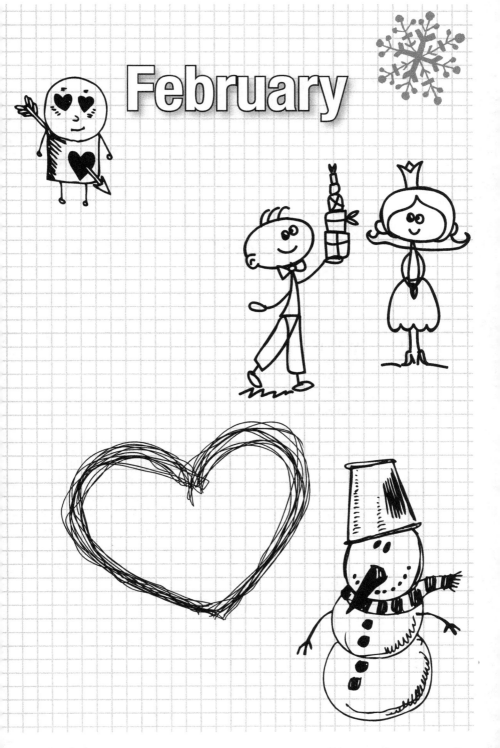

February

Finding Love

Sunday

"We have come to know and to believe in the love
God has for us. God is love, and whoever remains
in love remains in God and God in him....This is the
commandment we have from him: whoever loves God
must also love his brother" (1 John 4:16, 21).

God is love. Those who live in love live in God, and God lives in them,
but you must also love your brothers and sisters. Who are your "brothers and sisters" at school. Maybe you attend classes with them or share
meals and hang out with them on the weekends. God wants you to
love your extended family members and even those you disagree with.
When you love them with your whole heart, you make a commitment
to the best interest of that person, even if it means risking being hurt.
God wants you to watch out for each other. What can you do today to
be more loving? Taking care of your classmates is love.

Dear God,

Fill me with your love and I will try to extend it to everyone
I meet today, tomorrow, and every day thereafter. I love you,
Lord. Amen.

Monday

"God proves his love for us in that while we were still sinners
Christ died for us" (Romans 5:8).

Love conquers all. If a classmate, lab partner, or friend is insensitive, do not take it to heart. Let it go. In that situation, ask: What would Jesus do? If Jesus would let it go and love that individual, then you should, too. It takes too much energy to hold a grudge. Instead, let God's love flow around you. Love is the balm that soothes and heals. Reflect on times when you might have hurt someone. What did you do to seek forgiveness? If you do something against God's law, our Lord is quick to forgive, and opens a path for you to follow. He is such a kind and merciful God. How can you be more amicable and forgiving today?

Dear God,

Help me to let go of trivial grievances and past hurts. Free
me from the bonds that held me down for so long and teach
me to be more forgiving as I move forward with my life. Keep
me in tune to your love so I can touch everyone's heart with
goodness, happiness, and peace. Amen.

Tuesday

"The heart of the wise makes for eloquent speech, and
increases the learning on their lips" (Proverbs 16:23).

Think, then pray before you speak. Have you ever been caught off-guard and didn't know what to say to someone? Have you ever felt dismayed by someone's comments and unable to reply or offer a clever response? When that happens, ask the Holy Spirit to fill you with tranquility so your awkwardness diminishes and understanding prevails. In that way, you can sort out the good, overlook the bad, and act intelligently. God gave you an amazing mind that is capable of doing anything you want it to. Use it wisely and learn from the experience. Pray about it and God will tell you what to say and do. Saint Bernardine of Siena was a Franciscan priest who preached about God's love and mercy, peace and reconciliation. Initially his voice was hoarse and weak, but after prayer, it became robust and powerful. He is the patron saint of public speaking.

Dear God,

Remind me to take a deep breath and mull over my thoughts before I speak. Help me to be kind and persuasive for the good of all. Amen.

Wednesday

"Though the mountains fall away and the hills be shaken,
my love shall never fall away from you" (Isaiah 54:10).

In discouraging moments, God is there. Have you ever felt like your world was crumbling around you? Think about the last time you felt disheartened. How did you get through it? In your darkest hour, God is there waiting to embrace you in his infinite love. God is so huge that your brain cannot cognitively wrap around all of it. Love him continuously and unconditionally as he loves you. It is easy to love God when everything goes right: your friendships are harmonious, your classes go smoothly, and laughter comes easily. It is equally essential to love God when things go awry. Reflect on the last time something didn't go the way you expected and search for the good that was hidden in it. You might not immediately discover it, but it is there. Contemplate ways you can seek God amidst the chaos at school. How will you envelop God's rapture today on campus?

Dear God,

I want to love you with the same intensity as your love for me, even when things don't go as planned. Amen.

Thursday

"You answer us with awesome deeds of justice,
O God our savior, the hope of all the ends of the earth
and of those far off across the sea" (Psalm 65:6).

Eliminate the obstacles in your path. There are so many distractions at school: someone's music and laughter, an incoming text message, the desire to check social media or shop online, video games, the desire to go out. When you cannot focus, ask for God's help to concentrate.

If you cannot remove the diversions or ignore the interruptions, can you find a quiet place to study, learn, and pray? Can you go to the library? Whatever refuge you decide to work within, plan to stay until your assignments are complete. God wants you to be successful. Seek God first. Ask him to guide you around the hindrances that keep you from your work. Keep your spirituality in check and perhaps then, everything else will fall into place.

Dear God,

I place you before everything I must do today. You are the reason for my existence, my successes, and accomplishments. With you I know I can do anything. Your Son is my Savior. Amen.

Friday/Saturday

"For where two or three are gathered together in my name, there am I in the midst of them" (Matthew 18:20).

God is omnipresent. Believe in God and he will always be in your heart. God is also in the church community. Do you celebrate Mass with your classmates in a campus ministry or do you attend Mass off campus? It is good to pray to God alone, but it is also worthwhile to pray in a community of believers. When you study from a book, you will inevitably learn something. But it is more exhilarating to expand your educational experience in a classroom filled with other eager students who are interested in the same subject. Participating in a church service will make the experience of knowing and learning about God, and sharing his message, more meaningful. Do you ever consider skipping Mass? What are other valuable methods you use to connect with God? Do you pray with friends? Have you ever felt God's presence when you prayed in a group setting? Reflect on avenues for you to reach God in a deeper, more significant way.

Dear God,

Touch my heart and show me how to walk in your light. Amen.

Perseverance

Sunday

"I bless the LORD who counsels me;
even at night my heart exhorts me" (Psalm 16:7).

Calm yourself and talk to Jesus. What is the most tranquil spot
on your campus? Find a quiet place where you can meditate today.
Remove noises, distractions, and obtrusive thoughts from your head.
Draw near to God and ask him to speak to you. He will fill your heart
with peace and guide you through today and as you continue on your
collegiate journey. Do not get discouraged if you cannot hear him immediately. It's understandable to be so involved in your daily activities
and sometimes takes a while to hear God's messages. God is always
there with you and is inviting you to declutter your head and heart in
order to listen. What is the best time and place for you to pray? What
can you do to clear your mind to make room for the Lord?

> Dear God,
>
> Enable me to discover the classroom of silence. Open my
> ears, Lord, so that I can hear you. Help me to make sense of
> my life and how to serve you. I am ready, willing, and able.
> Amen.

Monday

"The LORD will fight for you; you have only to keep still"
(Exodus 14:14).

God has your back. Do you have a bodyguard? In anxious moments,
God has your back, to help carry you through struggles. Have you
felt the weight of the world bearing down on you this semester? What
courses do you enjoy the most and which are giving you grief? Turn to
God, who will reach down, pick you up, and dust you off. Do you have

the courage to give your problems to God? Saint Ignatius of Loyola was a Spanish knight who gradually transformed himself into a holy man through spiritual exercises. He believed emotions and feelings helped to understand the action of the spirit within to discover God's will. Can you create your own spiritual exercise, evaluating your feelings, in order to decipher God's will for you? In 1539, Ignatius formed the Society of Jesus and chose to live a life of poverty, chastity, and obedience. He is the patron saint of education.

Dear God,

Help me to recognize and appreciate your will for me.
Help me to grow spiritually and to know you wholly and completely. Amen.

Tuesday

"When God saw by their actions how they turned from
their evil way, he repented of the evil he had threatened
to do to them; he did not carry it out" (Jonah 3:10).

Seeking improvement pleases God. College students expand their minds by taking classes. Studying and doing projects for extra credit demonstrates your dedication to further advancement. What do you do for academic enhancement? Do you waste time perusing the Internet, playing video games, or watching TV? Reflect on ways you can perfect your productivity inside and outside of the classroom. Do you eat well-balanced meals, exercise, and get enough sleep? How do you perfect your faith? It pleases God when you try to improve your spirituality. God wants you to constantly work on refining yourself. Your soul is your most valuable possession. How will you cultivate it in your mind, heart, and entire being?

Dear God,

Teach me to nourish my mind, heart, and soul so that I can
strive to be the person you created me to be. Thank you for
the many gifts you have given me. I appreciate them and
the gift of faith that you grant to me, dear Lord. I love you.
Amen.

Wednesday

"Whoever ponders a matter will be successful;
happy the one who trusts in the LORD" (Proverbs 16:20).

Learning leads to success. When you attend class, do you pay attention or do you daydream and text friends? Have you ever skipped class without a reason? God provides the skills and tools necessary to learn and grow. Teaching assistants, tutors, and professors often post office hours for you to ask about extra help. Visit your university's learning center for more options. In addition to your studies and work, God wants you to find enjoyment in your life, too. What do you do for fun? Do you go to the movies or out for pizza? Ask God to help you find a happy balance in your life and to make room for spiritual growth. Ask for the courage to reject unhealthy outlets and make changes to keep you on the right track. What can you do today to expand your knowledge of God? Open your laptop and do a search for God. There is so much you can learn.

Dear God,

When my mind begins to wander, keep me focused.
I want to understand everything in my course work
so I may grow in your love. Amen.

Thursday

"In the same way, the Spirit too comes to the aid of our
weakness; for we do not know how to pray as we ought,
but the Spirit itself intercedes with inexpressible groanings"
(Romans 8:26).

Let the Holy Spirit work in you. How glorious it is to be reminded that during our weakest moments, the Holy Spirit is within us and intervenes for us. Can you turn yourself over to God and let the spirit move you? The Holy Spirit can enlighten and empower you as you go to and from classes today. Open your heart to be saturated with God's divinity and love to help you through every situation. What is on your agenda today that will enable you to rely on God's help? Take a few moments to quiet yourself and dwell on God's love for you. How will you show God that you love him? Remove all distractions so that you can focus on what is at hand, speaking in truth and love today and every day.

Dear God,

Fill me with the Holy Spirit and enable me to do my very best work today. I ask this in your sweet and holy name, Lord Jesus. Amen.

Friday/Saturday

"I will lead the blind on a way they do not know;
　　by paths they do not know I will guide them.
I will turn darkness into light before them,
　　and make crooked ways straight.
These are my promises: I made them,
　　I will not forsake them" (Isaiah 42:16).

What path are you on? Sometimes the Lord takes you down uncertain paths that you might question. You might even wonder how you arrived there. How did you choose your curriculum? What's the right one: biology, business, psychology, computers, engineering, agriculture, language, etc? Trust in God that he led you to your university for a reason. Though you might want to question that reason, God knows what he is doing. You are safe in his hands. How strong is your faith? Are there other avenues God has guided you toward? How do you see God's hand working in your life? The Lord will open pathways and guide you to the place he meant for you to be. Once you arrive, gladness will fill your heart.

Dear God,

Open my eyes and lead me to the place where you want me to be.
I trust you, Lord. Amen.

Take Control

Sunday

"Then I saw an angel come down from heaven,
holding in his hand the key to the abyss and a heavy chain"
(Revelation 20:1).

Angels safeguard you. Can you imagine having a combat Marine bodyguard at school? Angels are like mighty soldiers, keeping you safe. Do you feel invincible walking across your campus knowing you have an angel of the Lord protecting you? When you feel yourself being tempted, ask your guardian angel for fortification to enable you to do what is good and right. The Lord himself was tempted by the devil. The devil clashed with Anthony the Great (ca. 251–356), a holy monk, frustrating him with boredom and laziness, but he overcame these temptations with prayer. Satan reappeared as wild beasts and snakes. When Saint Anthony laughed at them, they disappeared in smoke. Saint Anthony was a hermit who lived in the desert, cut off from civilization. His love and devotion to God was steadfast. He is the patron saint of skin diseases and is known as the Father of all Monks.

Dear God,

Thank you for providing an angel to help me stay strong.
Envelop me in your grace, love, and mercy every day
of my life. Amen.

Monday

"Trust in the LORD with all your heart, on your own
intelligence do not rely; in all your ways be mindful of him,
and he will make straight your paths" (Proverbs 3:5–6).

Put God in control. Have you ever attended a class where the subject matter was beyond your comprehension and you did not understand anything the professor was teaching? Some topics are mind-boggling. Perhaps it was listening to skeptical friends explain why they are atheists or don't believe in miracles. Have you wondered who receives miracles? God does not expect you to understand, for these are beyond anyone's comprehension. God only wants you to accept and trust completely and absolutely. It is imperative to seek God in everything you say, think, and do. If you are able to do this, God will guide you through life. Your advisors can guide you through your studies, but it is the Lord who instructs and navigates your life. With God in the driver's seat, the sky is the limit. Who is in control of your life?

Dear God,

Expand my mind so I can understand my life journey
and all that is expected of me academically and spiritually.
Thank you for my intellectual capabilities and my ability
to love. Amen.

Tuesday

"I am your servant; give me discernment
that I may know your testimonies" (Psalm 119:125).

Be God's servant. College students often feel bombarded by work. Do you feel like work is all you do? What can you do for a healthy diversion? You likely selected your college because it had the best program for your particular course of study. Now it's your opportunity to learn everything about your desired major. Delve into your course work like it is the very essence of your being. Talk to your advisor about branching out into closely related fields or programs that you never considered before. Ask God to bless you with wisdom. One way you can learn more about your program is to actually work in that field of study. Perhaps you can volunteer or do an internship during the summer or while on a school break. Or you might go on a spring-break service trip with your campus ministry group. By working with the needy, we get to know God better. How can you be a servant to the Lord and understand his teachings?

Dear God,

Bless me with wisdom. Help me to find time to read
your word and get to know you better, too. I love you,
Lord, for all that you do for me. Amen.

Wednesday

"Rejoice, O youth, while you are young and let your heart be
glad in the days of your youth. Follow the ways of your heart,
the vision of your eyes; yet understand regarding all this that
God will bring you to judgment" (Ecclesiastes 11:9).

God wants you to enjoy life. You have the freedom to come and
go as you please, with activities and clubs you would not have the
opportunity to participate in at home. You have raves, concerts, and
themed parties to attend. It's wonderful to be a college student. What
do you enjoy the most about being a college student? You can explore
your options and pursue dreams. Be mindful that in doing so, God
holds you accountable for the choices you make. You won't be judged
for having fun and enjoying your life. Do you pray before deciding
how to spend your time? Ask God to bless your recreational activities.

Dear God,

Thank you for giving me these valuable and enjoyable college
experiences. I want to have fun and do well in my courses so
that some day soon I can do your work and please you all of
the days of my life. Amen.

Thursday

"Look, God is great, not disdainful;
his strength of purpose is great" (Job 36:5).

God understands everything. When you walk to class, who do you
talk to? Do you meet friends and stroll across campus together, or do
you talk on the phone, text, or tweet? Perhaps you listen to music on
an Mp3 Player. As you go to class today, unplug your electronic devices
and instead of talking to friends, talk to Jesus. Keep your heart open

so that you tune into to God's channel. Smile at the people who pass by because God is in each and every one. As you meander around campus today, listen to God's voice and ask for understanding so that you can appreciate his messages. God understands everything you carry in your heart.

Dear God,

Be near me as I give myself over to you. I need to feel your presence in my life more. Help me to eliminate distractions so that I can hear your voice, understand your message, and do your work. I want to live by your word. Work through me, Lord. I am here ready to serve. Please tell me what to do today. Amen.

Friday/Saturday

"Let your life be free from love of money but be content with what you have, for he has said, 'I will never forsake you or abandon you.' Thus we may say with confidence: 'The Lord is my helper, [and] I will not be afraid. What can anyone do to me?'" (Hebrews 13:5–6).

Give your troubles to God. Sometimes, college life with all of its classes and homework can feel more like a battle than a journey. You might have to fight your way through certain assignments, exams, or pesky interruptions. Perhaps you have a roommate or relationship conflict. Whatever your tribulations are, remember that God is with you through it all and will never turn his back on you. Turn over all your worries and problems to God. Ask him to help you to make sound decisions. Ask God to guide every step you take. What can you do today to show God you trust him?

Dear God,

Help me to submit to your plan by trusting totally in you. Teach me to always turn to you. Put your sweet name on my lips and let it live in my heart eternally. Amen.

Rejuvenation

Sunday

"As to more than these, my son, beware. Of the making
of many books there is no end, and in much study there
is weariness for the flesh. The last word, when all is heard:
Fear God and keep his commandments, for this concerns
all humankind" (Ecclesiastes 12:12–13).

Let God erase your confusion. Have you ever studied so much that
after a few hours you must close the books because you are more confused than ever? It's OK to be confused. You are human and expected
to occasionally feel bewildered. When this happens, turn to God.
While you need to do well in school, it is imperative to keep God's
commandments. How can you remember that your purpose on earth
is to live by God's golden rule? Is what you are doing at school pleasing
to God? If it is, the veil of confusion will lift and you will find your way.

Dear God,

I cry out to you in my confused state. Erase the mysteries
that have clouded my mind. Lift the fog and allow me to
focus on pleasing you, dear Lord. Amen.

Monday

"The apostles gathered together with Jesus and reported
all they had done and taught. He said to them, 'Come
away by yourselves to a deserted place and rest a while'"
(Mark 6:30–31).

Find relief in God's endless love. Do you get carried away in work by
studying constantly and being so absorbed with assignments that you
forget to take a break? What do you enjoy doing during study breaks?
Do you take naps, go for a walk, or shoot hoops? Take time to rest. Ask
God to bless your leisure so that you can be refreshed to work more
productively. Rest is just as important as work. Without relaxation,
you will wear yourself down and not work as efficiently. You cannot
run two marathons back to back without a break, but are in need of
a period of rest after the first one. Can you obtain relaxation during
prayerful moments? How will you squeeze rest and prayer into your
schedule today and throughout your week?

Dear God,

Help me to realize the importance of rest so that I do it today
between all of my assignments. Bless my rest so I can be more
productive as I work. Amen.

Tuesday

"Love is patient, love is kind. It is not jealous, [love] is not
pompous, it is not inflated, it is not rude, it does not seek its
own interests, it is not quick-tempered, it does not brood
over injury, it does not rejoice over wrongdoing but rejoices
with the truth. It bears all things, believes all things,
hopes all things, endures all things. Love never fails"
(1 Corinthians 13:4–8).

Who do you love? God spells out the message of how healthy love
needs to be. Are you in a relationship with someone? God knows what
your heart longs for. Ask Jesus to bless you with the right person who is
easygoing and will offer a kind and tender love. If this is not the right
time to meet this special person, ask for the patience to keep waiting
until the right time arrives for you to meet this individual. Can you
trust God that he knows what is best for you?

Dear God,

Thank you for putting many wonderful people in my life to love and appreciate. Help me strengthen those relationships and appreciate the companionship and love they offer. It's a gift, and I'm so glad I have it. Amen.

Wednesday

"Your kindness should be known to all. The Lord is near. Have no anxiety at all, but in everything, by prayer and petition, with thanksgiving, make your requests known to God. Then the peace of God that surpasses all understanding will guard your hearts and minds in Christ Jesus" (Philippians 4:5–7).

Ask God for what you need. What are your cares? Are you concerned about your assignments, time constraints, and grades? Worrying is a waste of time and energy. Instead, could you pray? Though worry gets you nowhere, prayer will help you move mountains. Tell God about your qualms and fears, and he will help you through it if your heart is thankful and peaceful. In your prayerfulness, thank God for all of the blessings and difficulties he has given you. In all things, goodness will come if you allow God to work in you. What will you thank God for? How will you demonstrate kindness and peace today?

Dear God,

Fill me with your love through prayer so that I focus on you and not my worries. I trust in your plans for my life, sweet, kind, and merciful Lord in heaven. Amen.

Thursday

"But the LORD said to Samuel: Do not judge from his appearance or from his lofty stature, because I have rejected him. God does not see as a mortal, who sees the appearance. The LORD looks into the heart" (1 Samuel 16:7).

God knows your heart. What is your favorite basketball team? The tall players might be champions on the court, but how will God judge their hearts? How will God judge your heart? As you walk past students on campus, do not judge or be distracted by designer labels on their clothes, tattoos, or body piercings. How can you identify their good qualities, their potential, and the kindness in their hearts? Do not be judgmental of your classmates. Underneath their many layers is a person a lot like you. What do you have in common with them? How can you be less judgmental of your classmates' outer appearances?

Dear God,

Help me to see into my classmates' hearts and
find the integrity and love that is hiding there.
Teach me to be more like you. Amen.

Friday/Saturday

"God did not give us a spirit of cowardice but rather
of power and love and self-control" (2 Timothy 1:7).

The Holy Spirit fills you with power, love, and self-control. Have you ever averted your professor's glance to avoid being spoken to? Has a scholarship deadline passed without you applying for it because you were afraid you wouldn't get it? Are you undecided about a decision because you fear the results? When you feel anxious, ask the Holy Spirit for help with whatever is stressing you out. This alertness will enable you to be cautiously optimistic instead of acting rashly or with regret. Don't let fear stagnate you, but make a prayerful decision by using the determination and wisdom that God gave you. Perhaps it means finding the resolution to say the right thing or the courage to walk away. How will you rely on the Holy Spirit over the weekend?

Dear God,

Thank you for teaching me that it is OK to remove myself
from a situation that causes me angst. Thank you for filling
me with the wisdom I need to make good decisions. Thank
you for helping me on my collegiate journey with bountiful
heavenly gifts, Lord. Amen.

March

Lent

Sunday

"All things are wearisome, too wearisome for words. The eye is not satisfied by seeing nor has the ear enough of hearing" (Ecclesiastes 1:8).

What is your investment? You are invested in your future by wanting to learn, discover, and grow. Think about all you have done to reach this point in your life. If you are willing to invest your time, energy, and money into your education, your ears should be motivated to listen to lectures and your eyes excited to read books. That is how the disciples felt when they were learning about the kingdom of God. Delve into your studies with the same enthusiasm as the apostles. How motivated are you to grow academically and spiritually? What have you invested in your spirituality to ensure you are going to heaven? What can you do during Lent to cleanse your soul and draw closer to God?

Dear God,

Open my mind completely to absorb the knowledge necessary to do your work here on earth. Erase all distractions. Clear a path for me to follow in your footsteps. I want to please you and serve you all the days of my life. Amen.

Monday

> "Remind people of these things and charge them before
> God to stop disputing about words. This serves no useful
> purpose since it harms those who listen" (2 Timothy 2:14).

Words are gifts; use them wisely. Have you had or overheard disagreements with someone at school? Does it really matter who is right or wrong? You do not have to win every argument. Agree to disagree. Words can make or break a relationships depending on what is said. Think about the message you want to convey to your advisor, roommate, or lab partner. Is someone being unfair? What will you do about it? Consider the words, manner, and tone Jesus would use. If Jesus were to speak for you, what do you think he would say? Ask the Holy Spirit to help find the right words to effectively communicate your messages so that there are no misinterpretations. This Lent, how can you work to avoid hurt feelings in your own relationships?

Dear God,

Fill my head with the ideas and notions to effectively
communicate my messages to the people at school.
I believe in you, dear Lord. Amen.

Tuesday

> "With your counsel you guide me,
> and at the end receive me with honor" (Psalm 73:24).

Make the best of college. It is an exciting notion that God is leading you to a glorious place. He knows your future and will help you get there. He has constructed a magnificent plan, and part of it involves attending college. Do you ever question that you are at the right school or in the correct program? What is causing your ambivalence? Do you feel camaraderie among classmates? When students are adorned in school colors, T-shirts, and sweatshirts with the school emblem and mascot, do you feel you belong? What do you wear to let God know you belong to him? College is not easy, but God will help you through it. He will bring you to a place of peacefulness and love. Make the most of your college experiences by trusting in the Lord.

Dear God,

Help me to trust in your plan. It is unnerving not knowing what it is. Sometimes it is difficult to be faithful, but I will do whatever you want me to. Lead me, guide me, and mentor me. You are my rock and my salvation. Amen.

Wednesday

"Your adornment should not be an external one: braiding the hair, wearing gold jewelry, or dressing in fine clothes, but rather the hidden character of the heart, expressed in the imperishable beauty of a gentle and calm disposition, which is precious in the sight of God" (1 Peter 3:3–4).

God cares about your inner beauty. Do you dress beyond your means, or do you take pride in your individuality regardless of your attire? God wants you to be yourself at school. He does not want you to pretend to be better than others. Do you know someone who acted superficially for acceptance into a club or group activity? Perhaps she did something she normally wouldn't do. Overlook flamboyant designer labels and high-tech toys flaunted by peers. Those things will not impress God. Instead, reflect on ways you can delight God. How do you appreciate your friends' inner beauty? What can you do during Lent to stop being judgmental of what classmates wear or don't wear?

Dear God,

Everyone has her own unique beauty. Help me to see it, Lord. Thank you for molding me into the person I am today. I adore you and love you. Amen.

Thursday

"Do you not know? Have you not heard? The LORD is God from of old, creator of the ends of the earth. He does not faint or grow weary, and his knowledge is beyond scrutiny. He gives power to the faint, abundant strength to the weak" (Isaiah 40:28–29).

Let God help you. Have you ever been overwhelmed with problems that you could not solve? Maybe you were stuck on a homework assignment or encountered difficulty fulfilling a Lenten obligation. Sometimes the best thing you can do is step away from it temporarily. Go for a walk, take a shower, or find a place where you can be alone with God. Stop trying to work through all of your problems on your own, but let God assist you. No one is bigger and stronger than God. It is possible that he will bring the perfect solution to your mind, or put the right person in your path to help you. During the season of Lent, how will you rely on God and hear his responses to the questions you ask?

Dear God,

Remind me that nothing will happen today that we can't handle together. Thank you for always being near. Amen.

Friday/Saturday

" 'What you are doing is not wise,' Moses' father-in-law
replied. 'You will surely wear yourself out, both you
and these people with you. The task is too heavy for you;
you cannot do it alone' " (Exodus 18:17–18).

Stop trying to do everything. With so many different classes, clubs, activities, and organizations, it's tempting to want to participate in all of them. Perhaps you signed up to chair a committee or event at school and realized it is too much work. Are you spreading yourself too thin? Choose between the ones that will bring you the most satisfaction, or delegate some of the work to your classmates. It takes boldness to speak up to request help. If you continue on your current path, you could burn yourself out, which would be disastrous. Know when to scale back on activities and clubs, and start saying "no thank you" to people when necessary. Realistically, you cannot do everything. Ask God for help. How will you turn to God during uncertain moments?

Dear God,

Teach me to accept and share my burden at school so that
I can be a much better person to everyone around me.
I love you. Amen.

Spiritual Growth

Sunday

"Those to whom God gives riches and property, and grants
power to partake of them, so that they receive their lot and
find joy in the fruits of their toil: This is a gift from God.
For they will hardly dwell on the shortness of life, because
God lets them busy themselves with the joy of their heart"
(Ecclesiastes 5:18–19).

Find joy in what you do. Fun events are built into the school calendar
where you can enjoy the camaraderie of classmates. God wants you to
find happiness and pleasure. It could be something simple, like listening to the chirping birds or the gladness you feel when the sun shines.
Francis of Assisi grew up wealthy but chose to live in poverty. He was
always happy regardless of what he had or didn't have. He found happiness in animals and in nature. What gives you joy? Take a moment
to thank God for all of the pleasures that he gives you.

Dear God,

Thank you for the many blessings you have given me. I am
fortunate to have this wonderful opportunity to learn, study,
and grow at college. Thank you, Lord, for helping me on this
journey. Amen.

Monday

"Fools take no delight in understanding,
   but only in displaying what they think" (Proverbs 18:2).

Pray for enlightenment. Do organizations you belong to schedule outings on Sundays because attending Mass is not a priority for them? Has a work-study program scheduled your hours during Mass time? How difficult is it for you to attend Mass on campus? Ask God to grant you the strength and wisdom necessary to understand the opinions and viewpoints of the teachers and students that conflict with your beliefs. Keep an open mind so that you can accept the truth, whatever it is. Don't be intolerant of your classmates. How do you quell your prejudices to avoid being hurtful toward them? Saint Thomas Aquinas promoted and advocated tolerance of unbelievers. How can you remember this scholarly saint the next time you need to practice open-mindedness at school? What can you do today to be more tolerant of other people's differences and beliefs?

Dear God,

Soften my heart so I can appreciate all feelings and
experiences that are different from what I believe.
Enable me to learn in this environment to exercise tolerance.
Thank you, Lord, for helping me to grow in your love. Amen.

Tuesday

"We love because he first loved us" (1 John 4:19).

Does God come first in your life? If so, everything else will fall into place. It may take a while or not be exactly the way you thought it would. Everything that happens does so because God intended it that way. He wants you to love others unconditionally, the way he loves you. If you want more love in your life, give some of your heart away. How can you do that? Stop for a moment to reflect on those individuals at your school who might need extra attention and care. What are small ways you can show someone that you care? Tell the Lord how much you love him. This brings such joy to his heart and will bless you immeasurably. Love is the best gift that you can give; and like a boomerang, whatever you give will come right back to you.

Dear God,

Allow me to understand and accept my life and the love that you are generating in me. I believe in your plan because I trust in you. I love you, Lord. Amen.

Wednesday

"There are friends who bring ruin, but there are true
friends more loyal than a brother" (Proverbs 18:24).

Friendships are gifts from God. Some friendships do not last, but some friends are more loyal than a sibling. It is wonderful to have trustworthy friends. You might see them in your classes, dining halls, at the gym, socials, and dormitories. Isn't it great to walk across campus and say, "hey!" to so many people you know and like? It feels nice when people smile back and say your name when you meet. What could be better than to have these people as lifelong friends? God blessed you with these special individuals to share in your joy and comfort you when you're down. Jesus is another friend you can always count on. He will always be there for you in good times and bad. What kind of friend are you to Christ? How can you show him you care?

Dear God,

Thank you for enriching my life with friends. Teach me how to provide honorable camaraderie to them and a life of service, love, and devotion to you. Amen.

Thursday

"Who is wise enough to understand these things?
Who is intelligent enough to know them?
Straight are the paths of the LORD, the just walk in them,
but sinners stumble in them" (Hosea 14:10).

Make wise choices. There are many different demands that will be placed on you, vying for your time. Perhaps it might be a career club, sport, or spinning class that dominates your time and energy. Maybe friends, roommates, or classmates eat up your free time. How much time do you spend on social media, shopping, or playing games each day? Whatever monopolizes your time, be sure to seek balance in your life. Choosing to follow God is the wisest choice you can make. When you do this, all of the other choices will be simpler. What is your biggest time commitment? Is it problematic to allow time for daily prayer and Mass on Sunday?

Dear God,

Help me to make wise choices and use my time sensibly.
Allow me to make room every single day to honor you, Lord.
I ask this in your sweet and holy name. Amen.

Friday/Saturday

"The astute see an evil and hide, while the naïve
continue on and pay the penalty" (Proverbs 22:3).

Be prepared. If you were to meet the pope, would you plan what to say, what to wear, and how to act? It's wise to be prepared in college, too; it's imperative to take into consideration how the day, week, month, and semester will unfold. Perhaps you could review your final-exam schedule to make sure you are on track and won't be slammed with tests or projects. Wise students reevaluate their course syllabus and plan for tests and assignments accordingly. People who do not plan will be caught off-guard and be easily derailed by the difficult circumstances they encounter. One of the most important plans you can make is to include God in your everyday life so that you will have eternal life in heaven. God wants you to be prepared. What can you do today to enhance your spiritual growth?

Dear God,

Help me to make preparations for heaven today by being productive with my limited time on earth. Let me always include you in those plans by living, loving, and learning your ways. Amen.

Spring Break

Sunday

> "Ask and it will be given to you; seek and you will find;
> knock and the door will be opened to you" (Matthew 7:7).

Persevere in prayer. Have you asked God for something and then became discouraged by waiting for it to come? During that period, God wants you to continue asking, praying, and searching for it. Throughout that time you might evaluate the underlying motive for what you want. Perhaps you seek understanding in a class, a better grade, acceptance in a friendship, or a change in a relationship. While you wait, pray persistently. God will enlighten and bless you. Reflect on the recent requests you have made to God. Have you prayed consistently and wholeheartedly for it? How have you continued to seek this desire? Think about how Saint Joseph felt when he learned that Mary was pregnant. How tenacious and steadfast do you think his prayers and pleas were to God? During the upcoming feast of Saint Joseph, how will you honor the foster father of Christ and the patron saint of the worker?

Dear God,

Open my heart and soul to the message you are trying
to convey to me. I only want to do what is right. Amen.

Monday

> "Behold, I am sending you like sheep in the midst of wolves;
> so be shrewd as serpents and simple as doves....When they
> hand you over, do not worry about how you are to speak
> or what you are to say. You will be given at that moment
> what you are to say. For it will not be you who speak
> but the Spirit of your Father speaking through you"
> (Matthew 10:16, 19–20).

Jesus calls you to a deeper level of trust. When you trust wholly
and completely, God will provide the right words at the right time.
Confrontations are never easy, but with God's grace, your confidence
in the Lord will carry you through. Ask the Holy Spirit to fill you with
peacefulness and enlightenment. Perhaps you had a misunderstanding
with a classmate, friend, or instructor. How did you handle it? Can
you trust God to deliver the perfect words to convey your thoughts
and feelings in order to accomplish the intended purpose? How will
you achieve this?

Dear God,

Strengthen me during this difficulty. Fill my head with the
right words so that I convey the right messages and leave a
trail of tranquility, peace, love, and joy. Amen.

Tuesday

> "Above all, let your love for one another be intense,
> because love covers a multitude of sins" (1 Peter 4:8).

Love is the balm that heals. God says to maintain constant love
for one another. It is easy to love friends who are nice to you, but it
is difficult to love someone who has hurt you. Who is a challenge for
you to love? Instead of focusing on an injury, can you concentrate on
your own inner healing when a friend pardoned you or overlooked
a past indiscretion? Most injuries to friendships are not intentional.
Consider forgiveness as Jesus did when he hung on the cross. When
you love freely and completely, forgiveness will follow. Saint Rita's
husband was a violent, dishonest, and abusive man. She was an hon-

orable wife while she lived with his viciousness for eighteen years, but she converted and forgave him before his death. She is the patron saint of impossible causes. Could you ask Saint Rita to intervene on your behalf to enable you to forgive someone?

Dear God,

Please mend my brokenness and keep love alive inside of me. Help me, Lord, to be more like you: loving, peaceful, and merciful. Amen.

Wednesday

"Again I saw all the oppressions that take place under the sun: the tears of the victims with none to comfort them! From the hand of their oppressors comes violence, and there is none to comfort them! And those now dead, I declared more fortunate in death than are the living to be still alive. And better off than both is the yet unborn, who has not seen the wicked work that is done under the sun" (Ecclesiastes 4:1–3).

Ask God for enlightenment. Some people can rub you the wrong way. You might not see eye-to-eye with them because you do not agree with what they say or believe. Yet God has put them in your path for some reason—maybe to learn something, feel something, or do something. Focus on what it is about that person that God likes. Then you might learn to understand or appreciate them. Do you see God in someone on campus? What touches you about that person?

Dear God,

Allow me to see you in (_____) and love unconditionally as you do. Amen.

Thursday

"Do nothing out of selfishness or out of vainglory; rather, humbly regard others as more important than yourselves, each looking out not for his own interests, but [also] everyone for those of others" (Philippians 2:3–4).

Recognize and acknowledge the goodness in people. While it may not be the way some college students act, it's important for you to remain appreciative to those who have been kind to you. Appreciation tells people that you don't take them for granted. Perhaps the cleaning lady in your dormitory has never been thanked for keeping your building clean. Maybe you forgot to thank someone who sent you a care package or gave you a lead on a potential summer job. Who have you overlooked during your college stint? Is there someone in your life who has been a wonderful presence? Let him know how much he means to you. When is the last time you thanked God? Thank God today for the good gifts in your life, especially as you rest during spring break.

Dear God,

Permit me to see the people who have gone unnoticed for so long. Open my eyes, Lord. I want to acknowledge their kindness. Thank you, Lord, for teaching me to do the right thing. Amen.

Friday/Saturday

"Do not fear, you shall not be put to shame; do not be discouraged, you shall not be disgraced. For the shame of your youth you shall forget, the reproach of your widowhood no longer remember" (Isaiah 54:4).

Leave the past in the past. God washes away your sins when you ask for forgiveness. Pray to God who will help you move on without regret. He does not want you to live in the past by dwelling on mistakes. God knows your sorrows, struggles, and your future. He will help you journey onward. Take a moment to reflect on your past actions and ways you can bring the Lord closer to you. Mary Magdalene strayed from the right path, for Scripture tells us that seven demons were cast out of her. Jesus changed her heart with a glance that pierced her soul. Ultimately she accompanied Jesus on his journeys and led other women to also follow him. No remorse is too great for God.

Dear God,

Allow me to pick up my head and walk in your love with dignity. Give me your hand, light my path, and show me the way. I love you, Lord. Amen.

Rising Above Adversity

Sunday

"The LORD is my light and my salvation; whom should I fear?
The LORD is my life's refuge; of whom should I be afraid?"
(Psalm 27:1).

God is your protector. Have you ever participated in an evening
activity at school that was held outdoors where the lighting was inad-
equate? Perhaps you struggled to see as you walked back to your dorm
after studying in the library late at night. A gigantic LED floodlight
would enable you to see where you were going to get back to your
dorm safely. God wants to be that guiding light in your life. The Lord
will illuminate your path, show you the way, rescue you from danger,
and keep you safe. With God, there is nothing to worry about. As long
as you live by God's ways, he will protect you. God is with you when
you are studying, taking exams, walking across campus at night, and
sleeping soundly in bed. Think about the times you have been afraid
at school. What did you do about it?

Dear God,

Thank you for always safeguarding me on my college journey.
Thank you for shining your magnificent rays of light into my
world. Amen.

Monday

> "For God who said, 'Let light shine out of darkness,' has
> shone in our hearts to bring to light the knowledge of the
> glory of God on the face of [Jesus] Christ. We are afflicted
> in every way, but not constrained; perplexed, but not driven
> to despair; persecuted, but not abandoned; struck down,
> but not destroyed" (2 Corinthians 4:6, 8–9).

Don't quit. There will be times when the demands of school become so burdensome and you might feel like giving up. God will never give more than you can carry. When you find yourself overwhelmed, stop and wait for the dust to settle around you. When God takes something from your grasp, he's not punishing you but simply opening your hands to accept something better. If you are experiencing difficulties and you cannot hear God, turn off your phone and look within for the answers. In the stillness, you will find him and hear his voice. Where can you go to give your soul the silence it needs today?

Dear God,

Keep me strong and focused on you as I struggle through this disparity. I believe in you and love you, dear Lord. Amen.

Tuesday

> "Therefore, confess your sins to one another and pray for
> one another, that you may be healed. The fervent prayer
> of a righteous person is very powerful" (James 5:16).

Apologies allow for healing and forgiveness. It is never easy to admit guilt and offer an apology when you have wronged someone. Do you have the courage to face a problem and say, "I was wrong, and I am sorry?" Healing and forgiveness will follow in time. If you want your relationships to grow to reach a new level of trust, you need to admit when you are wrong and follow up with a plan to prevent it from reoccurring. Do this with friends, roommates, professors, family members, and with God. Take a moment for some soulful reflection. Is there someone you need to apologize to? What plan will you implement to stop it from happening again?

Dear God,

Fill me with courage to face my fears and admit when I am wrong. Remind me of the importance of introspection and help me to make a heartfelt apology to create room for healing, and give me the courage to see it through. Help me be like you: kind and merciful. Amen.

Wednesday

"Cast all your worries upon him because he cares for you" (1 Peter 5:7).

Give your worries and fears to God. It doesn't matter how trivial or enormous your reservations are. Are you stressed about a friend, class, or professor? What are your fears? Can you give that problem to God? He cares about you and is never too busy to listen to whatever is bothering you. Even though there are pressing matters in the world, you are a priority to God. To God, you are precious. Give your troubles to him, for he loves you and wants to help you. Reach out to Jesus who is reaching out to you. There are many ways he could do this. He might put someone in your path who is an expert on the issue that you are stressing over. God brings special people into your life at precisely the right moment to assist you in achieving your goals. How will you put your trust in God today?

Dear God,

I am surrendering my problem (_____) into your loving arms. I need your help and guidance in handling this issue in a constructive manner. Please, help me, dear Lord. Amen.

Thursday

"Wine is arrogant, strong drink is riotous;
none who are intoxicated by them are wise" (Proverbs 20:1).

Do not go against the Bible. Alcohol is on every college campus, but you don't have to consume it just because it's there. What are a few options that would keep you abusing alcohol but are still enjoyable? How can you focus on your reason for being at school? Make learning, growing, and expanding your horizons a priority. Do some of your friends drink on the weekends and expect you to? Do not cave into peer pressure. If the Bible says it is unwise to get drunk, then why do it? Saint Monica is the patron saint of alcoholics and abuse victims. She married a man with a violent temper, but maintained her sweet disposition, giving to the poor, and praying constantly. She ultimately converted him and her three sons, one of whom is Saint Augustine. Ask Saint Monica to intercede on your behalf.

Dear God,

Show me healthy and useful ways to spend my weekends on campus so that I am pleasing to you. Help me, God, to always walk down the path of righteousness. Amen.

Friday/Saturday

"He himself bore our sins in his body upon the cross, so that, free from sin, we might live for righteousness. By his wounds you have been healed" (1 Peter 2:24).

What are your complaints? Is there a classmate or friend who grumbles about a professor or unfair assignments? Perhaps he rants about work or lack of money. What do you say or do you as you listen? Are you taking a boring elective this semester or an extremely difficult course? Think about the ways you are striving to get through. The next time you struggle through a particular difficulty at school, remember how painful it was for Jesus to suffer through his crucifixion. Can you ask Jesus to help you endure challenges at school? Jesus wants you to live a life of righteousness, and he will do whatever it takes to ensure you are heading in the right direction.

Dear God,

Let me be reminiscent of Jesus' crucifixion to help me stay on the right path and lead a good life so I can spend eternity in heaven with God. Amen.

Harness Your Inner Strength

Sunday

"Give and gifts will be given to you; a good measure,
packed together, shaken down, and overflowing, will be
poured into your lap. For the measure with which you
measure will in return be measured out to you" (Luke 6:38).

Be God's boomerang. Look closely at all God has given to you. Then it might be easier to give to others. God has provided you with so many resources. Reflect on them and thank God for them all. He has showered you with countless blessings and goodness and desires you to share this goodness and joy with all around you. The more you give to others, the more God blesses and fills you with his glory and light. How will you reach out to someone today? Will you seek her in person or by social media? What will you give? Are you a good listener? What are some special ways that you could use to help someone in need?

Dear God,

Help me to be more generous with my time, talents, love,
and possessions. And thank you for continuing to bless me,
even when I might not deserve it. I truly love you, Lord. Amen.

Monday

"We hold this treasure in earthen vessels that the surpassing
power may be of God and not from us" (2 Corinthians 4:7).

God provides. You are like a fragile clay jar containing a great treasure. Your authority is from God and not from yourself. God has put miraculous and healing powers in your heart. It does no good just to possess them, as in order to ignite these gifts you must do good works. Contemplate your ordinary powers; can you see an imprint of God in them? Saint Bonaventure says to examine your abilities and consider how they are illuminated by God. He explains that memory, the ability to retain endless things, images eternity as it can only come from above. How has your memory helped you this year at school? What magnificent gifts has God given to you? How have you used them to help further your education this year; and what have you done to help those surrounding you? How could you do more today? Saint Bonaventure is known as the seraphic doctor, as he revealed God's love to others as divine fire.

Dear God,

Teach me how to be more giving. Work through me to bring comfort and love to others. Amen.

Tuesday

" 'For I was hungry and you gave me food, I was thirsty
and you gave me drink, a stranger and you welcomed me,
naked and you clothed me, ill and you cared for me,
in prison and you visited me' "(Matthew 25:35–36).

Do God's work at school. After Saint Vincent de Paul studied humanities and theology, he dealt with setbacks and managed to create many charities for the poor. Don't let hindrances keep you from doing God's work while you are enrolled in school. How can you incorporate charitable acts in your busy schedule? Could you get involved in community projects with classmates? Reassess your schedule and ask God for guidance on the right venue to volunteer. Reach out to someone in need. No matter how small, giving can make a great difference to someone.

Dear God,

Clear a path in my busy schedule so that I can do your work. Point me in the right direction and tell me what to do. I will answer your call. Amen.

Wednesday

"Therefore, I will always remind you of these things, even though you already know them and are established in the truth you have. I think it right, as long as I am in this 'tent,' to stir you up by a reminder" (2 Peter 1:12–13).

Be open-minded to God's reminders. How does God give you prompts? Reflect on the opportunities God has given you to embrace his love throughout the day. When you study, do you wonder what you will actually be able to recall during exams? Offer up the drudgery of studying to the Lord, and ask God to bless the time and energy you expend doing so. Also, ask him to bless your memory, that you will retain this knowledge and use it accordingly. God wants you to be successful and bring your college experience to fruition in the form of a future job. That way, you will be able to do God's work in totality. It will also ensure that all you are doing at your university will not be in vain.

Dear God,

Bless my study time. Make me productive and enable me to retain all that I learn today, tomorrow, and always. Amen.

Thursday

"Avoid profane and silly myths. Train yourself for devotion, for, while physical training is of limited value, devotion is valuable in every respect, since it holds a promise of life both for the present and for the future" (1 Timothy 4:7–8).

Train yourself to be godly. Physical training is good, but preparation for godliness is much better because it promises benefits in this life and in the life to come. Do you remember how long it took you to use a computer with different software? After a while it became second nature. Just as musicians, artists, and athletes train to develop their talents, Christians need to train to develop and enhance their spirituality. This can be done through prayer and random acts of kindness. If you work on developing your skills, God promises to reward you now and in heaven. What can you do today to cultivate yourself for godliness?

Dear God,

Increase my awareness to be more helpful to everyone
I encounter at this university whether I know that person
or not. I adore you, Lord. Amen.

Friday/Saturday

"It is good for a person, when young, to bear the yoke"
(Lamentations 3:27).

Learn patience. Perseverance is a lifelong skill that will always be needed. Throughout your life you will be faced with situations where you are required to wait. If you have a toothache, waiting for the dentist is agonizing. Waiting to get well after a cold or flu can also be unbearable. Waiting to find out if you passed or failed a test is not easy, either. Perhaps you are waiting for the semester to end and summer to begin. What wait have you recently made that you agonized over? How did you get through it? What can you do to acquire more patience in your life as a college student? Saint Thérèse of Lisieux was told she was too young to join the Carmelite convent and had to wait. After she finally became a nun, she experienced annoyances from the sisters she lived with. Instead of confronting them, she patiently endured the irritations and offered them to God. What can you do today to be more tolerant of others?

Dear God,

Teach me the patience of Saint Thérèse. Help me, Lord.
Amen.

April

Easter

Sunday

"Jesus himself drew near and walked with them, but their eyes were prevented from recognizing him" (Luke 24:15–16).

Know with whom you are walking. After a funeral, you don't expect to see that person again. Even though Jesus told his disciples that he would rise from the dead, they did not recognize him once they saw him. Have you ever wondered if you met Jesus walking across your campus, would you recognize him? How would you know for sure that it was Christ? When you meander around your college campus with a group of friends, how often do you think that the Holy Spirit is in each one of them? How can you plan to actively seek God in the people you encounter? On Easter Sunday, how will you rejoice in the resurrection of the Lord?

Dear God,

Thank you for everything you have done. You loved me so much that you sent your only Son, watching him suffer, die, and rise from the dead. Thank you for that sacrifice. Your love lifts me up and holds me next to you, dear Lord. I am so glad that I have you in my life. Amen.

Monday

"Your word is a lamp for my feet, a light for my path" (Psalm 119:105).

Know the Lord. When you decide between courses and electives to take, do you sign up without knowing anything about them? How do you educate yourself about them? Do you talk to students who have previously taken them, the professor teaching them, or to your advisor? Before you delve into a class, you should do some legwork. Likewise, before you can do God's work, first get to know him. The best way to do that is by praying, reading, and reflecting upon sacred Scripture. Then, God will guide and keep you on course. While it's critical to research classes and read schoolbooks, it's also important to read God's holy book. Put God first in your life, and really get to know him so that everything else will fall into order. Take a few minutes to reflect on God and his messages today.

> Dear God,
>
> Thank you for allowing me to learn about you while I am away from home. Without the support of my family and home parish, I am depending on your spiritual guidance now more than ever. Amen.

Tuesday

> "My son, if you receive my words and treasure my commands,
> Turning your ear to wisdom, inclining your heart to understanding. Then will you understand the fear of the LORD;
> the knowledge of God you will find. Then you will understand what is right and just, what is fair, every good path"
> (Proverbs 2:1–2, 5, 9).

Consecrate your consciousness to God. Are you familiar with the phrase, "it's who you know?" The Scripture infers how essential it is to know God, listen to his Word, and do what he says. While it is important to open your schoolbooks and study, it is equally important to open the Bible, read it, comprehend it, and live it. Keep your heart open and you will be able to decipher God's messages. Read his words and listen to his voice, and then act upon God's message. If you do this, God's infinite wisdom will provide you with right judgment.

Dear God,

Grant me the wisdom to understand your words so I know what you want me to do with my life. I am here to serve and please you, kind and merciful Savior. Amen.

Wednesday

"...Everything must be done properly and in order" (1 Corinthians 14:40).

Pray every day. Wouldn't it be nice if everything fell into place just right? Homework assignments pile up, professors make demands, and before long, you are backlogged. Strive to put your day back together and minimize wasteful time, especially as the end of the semester approaches. Make to-do lists and prioritize them. At the top of that list, write: PRAY. Keep a healthy balance between your classes, time for socialization, and spiritual reflection. What will you do for fun today? Perhaps before you begin your homework you could gather in a lounge with friends to discuss the events of your day or make weekend plans. Saint Alphonsus Liguori recommended people pray the way one talks to their friends. He suggested telling God about the events of your day and including your feelings. Can you try praying that way today? Saint Liguori left a legal career to join the priesthood and founded Evening Chapels.

Dear God,

Keep my life orderly. Reduce my stress and teach me to be more productive. Thank you for helping me to keep harmony in my life and find ways to honor and love you. Amen.

Thursday

"Blind guides, who strain out the gnat and swallow the camel!" (Matthew 23:24).

Only God is perfect. Jesus' sense of humor reminds you not to pick at your friend's faults. Take your eyes off your friend's problems and examine your own. If you think you do not have any flaws, ask your roommate or best friend. No one is perfect—except for God. Ask the

Lord to have mercy upon you and teach you how to be a better person and friend. Perhaps using your sense of humor, like Jesus did, will help you deal with your friend's imperfections and your own. Saint Philip Neri used practical jokes as a way to establish friendships. His happy-go-lucky disposition concealed his true emotions. Can you use this technique to overlook your friends' quirks? He founded the secular clergy called the Congregation of the Oratory.

Dear God,

Forgive me for finding faults with my friends and classmates. You are in each of them. When I pick at their flaws, I am hurting you, and I am sorry. Teach me to be lighthearted, to let negativity fall away from me and let me keep only what is positive and wonderful. Amen.

Friday/Saturday

"At that he began to curse and to swear, 'I do not know the man.' And immediately a cock crowed. Then Peter remembered the word that Jesus had spoken: 'Before the cock crows you will deny me three times.' He went out and began to weep bitterly" (Matthew 26:74–75).

Learn from a failed experience. Failure, as hard as it is, does not end your chances for success. It might feel that way, but it can be a lesson. You discovered a way that did not work. Try something else the next time. Though you could fail again, failure is inevitable and is not necessarily a bad thing. Saint Cyprian was a man with strong principles who was committed to his journey. Like you, he valued education. While he made mistakes, he regaled life living passionately. Don't fret over failure because it checks your pride, for it enables you to reexamine your methods, make corrections, and try again. Ironically, it wasn't until after Saint Peter's great failure that he truly succeeded as "Peter the rock." What disappointments weigh heavy on your heart? What can you learn from them?

Dear God,

Help me to accept my failures, learn from them, and to move on and continue to grow. Amen.

Redefine Who You Are

Sunday

> "That resourcefulness may be imparted to the naïve,
> knowledge and discretion to the young. The wise by hearing
> them will advance in learning, the intelligent will gain
> sound guidance, to comprehend proverb and byword,
> the words of the wise and their riddles. Fear of the LORD
> is the beginning of knowledge; fools despise wisdom and
> discipline" (Proverbs 1:4–7).

God is the foundation of knowledge. All of the information you receive passes through the filter of God's wisdom. God's words will enable you to be clever and resourceful. Ask God for guidance. When you struggle to find your purpose in life, look to God for the answer, and spend time getting to know the Lord who will reveal his purpose for you. How can you become better acquainted with God? Ask the Lord to bless your studies this week and see what happens!

Dear God,

Help me to be patient while I wait for you to reveal your master plan of my life to me. Help me to be accepting and enjoy it as it unfolds. Enable me to experience every second of it wisely so that it is pleasing to you. Amen.

Monday

> "A glad heart lights up the face, but an anguished heart
> breaks the spirit....A joyful heart is the health of the body"
> (Proverbs 15:13; 17:22).

Let God fill you with happiness. When you are happy on the inside, you will be happy on the outside. For joy bubbles out and spreads to those around you. Be less serious and find humor to lighten your day. Laughter is contagious and is also the best cure for whatever ails you. If you are feeling down because of test scores, GPAs, or loneliness, give these struggles to God and ask for enlightenment. Reflect on times when you felt blue about something but chose to change your attitude toward it. Did your positive outlook make you feel better? Did prayer factor into it? Search the depth of your heart for the love that God gave to you and perhaps that will fill you with the happiness you have been seeking.

> Dear God,
>
> Fill my heart with gladness today. Help me to smile so that I bring a ray to sunshine to everyone I meet. Keep my heart light, my soul bright, and my mind right. Amen.

Tuesday

> "Trustworthy are the blows of a friend,
> dangerous, the kisses of an enemy" (Proverbs 27:6).

Have an open mind and a pliable heart. Do you value your friendships? Has someone hurt you this year? Sometimes friends mean well when they inadvertently hurt you. Accept constructive criticism from friends who are looking out for your best interest. Receive their words with an open mind, contemplating the message and intentions, and pray for acceptance of their message. Foster the genuineness of your friendships. It took courage for your friends to approach you. Because your friends care about you, they refuse to remain silent. What can you learn from the messages your friends delivered? How can you work on self-improvement? Have you misinterpreted an unintentional hurt? How have you reached out to God during this difficult time?

Dear God,

I feel so vulnerable to heartache when my friends approach me on a topic that is difficult to hear. Soften their message and give me the strength to accept it and take action on it. Walk with me as I take the first step in the right direction. Help me to be resilient and grow in your eternal love. Amen.

Wednesday

"The LORD is my shepherd; there is nothing I lack. In green pastures he makes me lie down; to still waters he leads me; he restores my soul. He guides me along right paths for the sake of his name. Even though I walk through the valley of the shadow of death, I will fear no evil, for you are with me; your rod and your staff comfort me" (Psalm 23:1–4).

God is your rescuer. Ask God to eliminate distractions and allow you to focus on one subject at a time until you master it. Take proper nourishment to recharge before you study. In order to retain what you learned, your brain cells need energy. Do you take frequent breaks to pray? God will help you in your time of need. After exams, the price of studying will pay off and you will be rewarded with an honorable grade. Reflect on ways God has restored your soul in the past. What can you do to stay in good graces with God?

Dear God,

Make my study time productive. Bless me with knowledge and understanding to do well on tests and projects. Thank you, Lord Jesus, for always being there for me. Amen.

Thursday

"He raises the needy from the dust; from the ash heap lifts up the poor, to seat them with nobles and make a glorious throne their heritage. 'For the pillars of the earth are the LORD's, and he has set the world upon them. He guards the footsteps of his faithful ones, but the wicked shall perish in the darkness; for not by strength does one prevail" (1 Samuel 2:8–9).

God can raise you up. God is the bright sun shining through the dark clouds that loom overhead. Is the grind of schoolwork taking its toll and wearing you down? Close your books for a while and take a moment to pray. Go for a short walk and talk to the Lord. The fresh air will rejuvenate you. Look for signs of the Lord as you walk. He is there in the person who smiled at you. Can you feel him? Quiet yourself, remove every thought from your head, and focus on Jesus' face. Dwell on your loving Savior.

Dear God,

Open my heart so that I can be filled with your love as I focus only on you. You are my deliverer and I love you. Amen.

Friday/Saturday

"Do not let your hearts be troubled. You have faith in God; have faith also in me. In my Father's house there are many dwelling places. If there were not, would I have told you that I am going to prepare a place for you? And if I go and prepare a place for you, I will come back again and take you to myself, so that where I am you also may be" (John 14:1–3).

Surrender yourself to Jesus. He will take care of you. He provides comfort in this weary world full of stressful exams and projects with pending deadlines. No matter where you are physically, emotionally, or mentally, you can always turn to God and be at "home" with him. You will not find him on the Internet, and you cannot text or phone him, but you can call out his name anytime and anywhere. Reflect on occasions when you should have called out to the Lord but did not. How will you seek God now?

Dear God,

I lay my troubled heart at your feet seeking your consolation. Please help me, my Lord and Savior. Tell me what to do; and I will listen and obey. Amen.

Pursuit of Education, Wisdom, and Happiness

Sunday

"Many peoples shall come and say: 'Come, let us go up to the LORD's mountain, to the house of the God of Jacob, that he may instruct us in his ways, and we may walk in his paths.'" (Isaiah 2:3)

Get to know God. Have you ever struggled to translate a text message? Occasionally it can be difficult to decipher the intended message of the sender. Perhaps a word was spelled incorrectly or an essential word was missing entirely. God will not send a text or e-mail informing you of his wishes. Close your laptop and phone and tune into Jesus. You can seek out your life mission by praying, reading the Bible, and spreading God's word. Do you notice the people God puts in your path? Think about the people God has brought into your life. Has someone touched your heart recently? God is in each person you encounter. How will you get to know God better and understand the messages he wants you to be familiar with?

Dear God,

What is my mission? Open my eyes so that I can recognize you and do your work. I trust you and love you, Lord. Amen.

Monday

"From heaven the LORD looks down and observes the children of Adam, from his dwelling place he surveys all who dwell on earth. The One who fashioned together their hearts is the One who knows all their works" (Psalm 33:13–15).

God is in control. Are your professors piling on the work and does it appear unmanageable? Are too many demands being placed upon you? No matter how out of control your schoolwork seems, God has authority over all. Since God made you, he knows what you carry in your heart as well as the troubles that weigh heavily on your shoulders. Put your trust in God. While Saint Joan of Arc was a teenager, she led the French army to several victories through her implicit trust in the Lord. As you battle your way through your assignments, recall Saint Joan's determination that led her to be successful. What is weighing heavy on your heart? Can you give it to God and trust that he will enable you to work through it; if so, how?

Dear God,

Bring a semblance of order to my life. I trust in you,
dear Lord, to help me be successful in school. Amen.

Tuesday

"Many are the plans of the human heart, but it is
the decision of the LORD that endures" (Proverbs 19:21).

What is God's will for you? It is understandable to question God's master plan, especially if it is not apparent. Continue to make plans every day to stay on schedule with your course work. Have you ever attended a performance and wondered how such an event made it to the stage? Every performer did his part. At school, you need to do your part. Sometimes it's unsettling not knowing for certain what you need to do; but through spiritual reflection, God will enlighten you. How can you be open and accepting of what God asks even if you don't understand it? God's plans are vital and he will prevail. How will you get the courage to do God's will? When you do so, everything else in your life will mysteriously fall into perfect place. Ponder the times in the past where you might have ignored God. How will you listen for God's voice and respond?

Dear God,

Whatever you want me to do with my life, make me see it
more clearly. I want to please you and have a harmonious life
of endless service. Amen.

Wednesday

"How good and how pleasant it is,
    when brothers dwell together as one!" (Psalm 133:1).

Get along with your neighbors. It is not always easy to live with people you don't know that well in the dormitories. You might have to share bathrooms, kitchenettes, laboratories, or other academic platforms. What do you have to share in college and how is that working out? Is there anything you could do differently? People have different lifestyles and routines, morals and beliefs. Don't cave in to someone else's ways and behaviors, but be firm about your principles. It is important to find a way to get along with everyone and be agreeable while maintaining your own identity. It is good for the soul to work toward a happy relationship with your classmates. Reflect on past occasions where it was challenging to get along with someone. How did you get through that? What can you do in the future to ensure a harmonious environment to live within?

Dear God,

Keep me resilient as I live with (_____). Let me be a good role model with optimistic behaviors. I want to love everyone on my college journey. With your guidance, I will succeed. Amen.

Thursday

"I no longer call you slaves, because a slave does not know what his master is doing. I have called you friends, because I have told you everything I have heard from my Father" (John 15:15).

Friends are gifts from God. When you think about all of the friendships you have made at school, do you wonder about their qualities that are so endearing? Friends are gifts that God puts in your life to make it more enjoyable. Reflect on how you share your college experiences and the ways you grow with your friends. What are some of your qualities that make you so dear to God's heart? What have you done this semester that was especially pleasing to God? As your semester nears its end, how can you concentrate on developing your friendship further with the Lord? Will you keep in touch with your friends over the summer? How will you keep in touch with God?

Dear God,

Thank you for the friends you have placed in my path. Make me cognizant of the friendship I am developing with you, my sweet Lord. Amen.

Friday/Saturday

"Do not conform yourselves to this age but be transformed by the renewal of your mind, that you may discern what is the will of God, what is good and pleasing and perfect" (Romans 12:2).

Let hope keep you happy. Be patient and continue to pray. What are your difficulties? In the midst of them, turn to God for spiritual guidance to see beyond them. Being surrounded by unbelievers in your university setting can skew and influence your decisions; but strive not to let this happen. Perhaps you are exposed to their vulgar language, cutthroat competition, and gossip; but you also might be attracted to their personality traits. You can take necessary steps to stay resilient to negative behaviors by reading holy Scripture and talking to God. The Word of God cleanses the world's contaminations and provides a mystical suit of armor to allow for transformation into Christ's image, enabling us to influence others for the better. Prayer will bring Jesus close to you and is stronger and more effective than any weapon or tool you could use. God loves you and wants you to live in his love! What will transform you into Christ's image?

Dear God,

Life seems so complicated. Help me, Lord, to stay strong in your love. Amen.

Spiritual Renewal

Sunday

"Watch and pray that you may not undergo the test.
The spirit is willing, but the flesh is weak" (Matthew 26:41).

Be accountable. With so many demands being placed on you, it is plausible to drift from God at school. One day you might be too tired to pray, the next you might be overwhelmed with homework. Before you know it, you haven't opened your Bible in weeks. Have you ever skipped Mass because you were feeling lazy? Don't let those habits become the norm. How can you get back on track? With God on your side you will always walk the right path. Saint Norbert of Xanten lived a life of pleasure. He was transformed after a near fatal accident brought him to a life of penance. Don't wait for an accident to become reacquainted with the Lord. How do you plan to reach out to God today? This German saint founded the Abbey of Fürstenberg in 1115.

Dear God,

Fortify and enlighten me with your love, mercy, and spiritual graces. Empower me to stand up to the world's disillusionments and make wise choices about what is truly best for me. Amen.

Monday

"If I take the wings of dawn and dwell beyond the sea, even there your hand guides me, your right hand holds me fast" (Psalm 139:9–10).

God will never leave you. Studying at a university is a major undertaking packed with excitement and adventure. What are some of the experiences that your school has afforded you this year? Perhaps you learned a new language, became knowledgeable about a different culture, met interesting or different people, or decided to study abroad. Latch onto the university's wings and be carried wherever the prospects take you. Rest assured that while God expands your wings to fly, he is also holding on to you throughout the journey the same way your parents ran beside you when you learned to ride a bike. Only God has an endless stream of energy and will not let go. Reflect on where your spiritual journey has taken you. Today, notice God's hand navigating the opportunities you encounter. What are they?

> Dear God,
>
> My college experiences are both exciting and nerve-racking. Thank you for bringing them to me and for always being near to safeguard me. Amen.

Tuesday

> "Keep on doing what you have learned and received and heard and seen in me. Then the God of peace will be with you" (Philippians 4:9).

Strive to be your best because it pleases God. The first time you jog you cannot expect to run a marathon. It takes a great deal of practice to build up your strength and endurance. What have you dedicated time and energy to perfecting? Perhaps you want to excel in your schoolwork, bring up your GPA, improve in a sport, or play a musical instrument. What do you do to strengthen your faith? You also need to practice being a good Christian. What are some ways you could do that? Does your university reach out into the community? Are there charitable acts you could do? What are some helpful things you could do on campus? Could you tutor underclassmen or refugees in your neighborhood? Look for ways you can reach out to others because that is pleasing to God.

Dear God,

Be with me as I practice being a good Christian.
I want to do your work and please you, Lord. Amen.

Wednesday

"Consider this: whoever sows sparingly will also reap sparingly,
and whoever sows bountifully will also reap bountifully.
You are being enriched in every way for all generosity,
which through us produces thanksgiving to God"
(2 Corinthians 9:6, 11).

Be generous with what you have. God wants you to be charitable and share the blessings he has bequeathed to you. Whatever you give, God will return the goodness tenfold. God wants you to share everything: your time, talents, food, clothing, and riches. Pause for a moment to think about something you could share. Could you help a friend who is struggling to understand the concepts of an assignment? When you are considerate to your fellow classmates, God will shower you with much love and many blessings. What can you share today?

Dear God,

Teach me to give generously, for you have given so much
to me. Thank you for the countless blessings that you
have bestowed upon me. I feel enriched by your love.
Help me to give it away, for I know in your goodness,
you will return my gestures ten times over. I love you,
kind and compassionate Lord. Amen.

Thursday

"Jesus said to him, 'If you can!' Everything is possible
to one who has faith" (Mark 9:23).

Believe. If you question the plausibility of completing a project, course, or curriculum, have faith in God that he will see you through it according to his will. No matter how difficult the task is, if God wants it done, it will be completed. Do you ever second-guess your curriculum or course load? The path you are on is the one God chose for you. When Saint Antoninus wished to enter the Dominican house, he was told to first learn a book containing several hundred pages by heart. He did it within a year. Nothing is impossible with God if you believe. Instead of worrying about an assignment, give it to God. Ask him to ease your burden and bring you focus and enlightenment. That way you will have more room in your heart to love and honor God. How will you do that?

Dear God,

Please give me the stamina to continue working productively. When I get overwhelmed, I question everything. Take my doubt and replace it with your love. Amen.

Friday/Saturday

"The LORD looks down from heaven upon the children of men, to see if even one is wise, if even one seeks God" (Psalm 14:2).

First, honor God. It pleases God when he sees you praying, reading the Bible, and performing acts of service. It isn't easy to juggle your courses, homework, clubs, and activities. God knows your anguish and it pleases him to see you making an effort and taking time to pray throughout the day. If you want to be wise in school, don't just do what your professors want; also do what God wants. Saint Dominic felt a calling to a career in the church while he was a student. Dominic's love of learning was detailed in a story during his student days. While he treasured his books, he sold them for money for the poor. What can you do today to be more like Dominic?

Dear God,

Wash away my stress and worries so that I can pray with an open mind, free of clutter and guilt. Help me to get through my homework quickly so I can spend quality time reading the Bible tonight and getting better acquainted with you. Amen.

May

Conform to God's Standards

Sunday

"But the wicked are like the tossing sea which cannot be still, its waters cast up mire and mud. There is no peace for the wicked, says my God" (Isaiah 57:20–21).

Set a good example. You know who the rowdy students are; you hear and see them everywhere on campus. Often, all these lost souls need is a good leader to follow. Use your valuable time wisely and personify the best you can be while you attend school. How can you do this? Saint Bruno was well-educated and became the director of schools within his diocese. While working in that capacity, many enemies arose against him. He stood firm in his principles, denouncing their transgressions. Saint Bruno was exiled for standing up for righteousness. Can you invoke Saint Bruno's philosophies when you encounter the wrong crowd at school?

Dear God,

Give me the courage to walk away from unruly students. Their smiles and jovial nature are alluring, but I know my time is better spent in the library learning or reading the holy Scriptures. Arm me with the wisdom I need to walk the path of righteousness. Amen.

Monday

> "Avoid foolish and ignorant debates, for you know that
> they breed quarrels. A slave of the Lord should not quarrel,
> but should be gentle with everyone, able to teach, tolerant,
> correcting opponents with kindness. It may be that God will
> grant them repentance that leads to knowledge of the truth"
> (2 Timothy 2:23–25).

Don't get drawn into arguments. Avoid senseless controversies because they breed quarrels. Be kind to everyone, an apt teacher, patient, and correct opponents with gentleness. Walk away from squabbles and pray for the people involved in them. You will not share every viewpoint with your friends and classmates. How do you handle tense situations at school? Do you offer kind words to everyone you meet? Do you remain level-headed when an argument erupts? How do you think clearly and intelligently when conflict arises between you and a classmate? What can you do today to promote peacefulness on campus?

> Dear God,
>
> Fill me with love and compassion for everyone on my
> campus, especially argumentative people, obnoxious
> professors, and unpleasant students. Enable me to find
> something good in every person I meet. I ask this in your
> sweet and holy name. Amen.

Tuesday

> "Now to him who is able to accomplish far more than all we
> ask or imagine, by the power at work within us, to him be
> glory in the church and in Christ Jesus to all generations,
> forever and ever. Amen" (Ephesians 3:20–21).

God brings out the best in you. When you gaze at your reflection in the mirror, you might see an ordinary person or someone with flaws and limitations. When you look at yourself, are you happy with what you see? God overlooks any inadequacies and sees your full potential and your true inner beauty. When God looks at you, he sees more than you can imagine. You can do the Lord's work regardless of the obstacles in your path or the size of the task before you because God works through you. God's powers work within you to accomplish infinitely more than you might think. What monumental assignment are you facing that you fear you cannot do alone?

Dear God,

When I see my reflection, allow me to find you there. Grant me the wisdom to be satisfied with what I see. Help me to see my talents and the ability to use them to serve you; and give me the courage to do your work on this college campus, whatever that may be. Amen.

Wednesday

"You know when I sit and stand; you understand my thoughts from afar. Where can I go from your spirit? From your presence, where can I flee?" (Psalm 139:2, 7).

God is with you. While you are away from home, you have God's vigilant eye on you. Are you apprehensive when leaving a night class as you walk across the campus in the dark? What fears are unique to your college experience? Maybe you are anxious about imminent final exams or you don't have firm summer plans yet. Whatever your concerns are, God will hold your heart and carry you when the road becomes too difficult for you to walk. Think of Saint Xenia, who became severely depressed when her husband died. She gave her possessions to the poor and wandered the streets of Saint Petersburg, centering her life on God. She sought protection and comfort only from God. Can you depend completely on God to safeguard you the way this Russian saint did?

Dear God,

Wrap your loving arms around me by comforting and enlightening me while I study, learn, and grow in your unfaltering love. Amen.

Thursday

"Now then, speak thus to my servant David, Thus says the LORD of hosts: I took you from the pasture, from following

the flock, to become ruler over my people Israel. I was with
you wherever you went, and I cut down all your enemies
before you. And I will make your name like that of the
greatest on earth" (2 Samuel 7:8–9).

Know God to experience miracles. God can grant tremendous
greatness for others to see how magnificent he really is. God can select
you from an ordinary high school and put you in a wonderful learning
environment; and God can expand your mind to learn beyond your
wildest imagination so that some day you can do great things for humankind. This way, others might come to know God and experience
his miracles, too. Reflect on an occasion where God touched your life
in a miraculous way.

Dear God,

Come into my life and bring me to
the place you want me to be. Amen.

Friday/Saturday

"Fear of the LORD is the beginning of knowledge;
fools despise wisdom and discipline" (Proverbs 1:7).

Dedicate time to God. The professors at your university can tantalize
your brain by exposing you to information by unfathomable things
that you could have only dreamed of learning and doing before. This
knowledge can open doors for future employment and opportunities
that can take you to magnificent places. It is essential to study hard
and learn by your university's rules to ensure your future success.
Universities cannot teach you how to live intelligently, honestly, justly,
and fairly. Do not devote your time and energy only to your studies;
also read the Bible, pray every day, and do God's work. Think back to
your first day of classes and reflect on how much you have learned.
What role did God play in your ability to learn? How will you praise
God and ensure that he will always be a part of your life?

Dear God,

Enable me to make time to get to know you better
so that I can live an honest life in your love. Amen.

Stamina and Resolution

Sunday

"Each one must examine his own work, and then he will have reason to boast with regard to himself alone, and not with regard to someone else; for each will bear his own load" (Galatians 6:4–5).

Do your own work with God's blessing. Test your work; then it will become a basis for pride. Have you been tempted to submit less-than-perfect homework? Are you exhausted from the grueling workload? Are you looking for shortcuts? Perhaps you want to blow off steam instead of studying. You might even second-guess your future and question why the courses you are taking matter. In the end, you will be proud of your accomplishments and be glad that you did not compromise your integrity. Turn to God in your struggles, asking the Lord to bring clarity and resolution to your situation. How will you take pride in all you have accomplished this semester? How can you offer up your work and diligence to the Lord?

Dear God,

Bless my work and all that I do today. Shower me with your love so that I can fearlessly approach my day and accomplish all I must do. I offer my suffering to you, dear Lord. Amen.

Monday

> "To you they cried out and they escaped;
> in you they trusted and were not disappointed" (Psalm 22:6).

God is working in your life. There will be disappointments in college. It could be receiving an unjust grade or unfair assignment. It could be through changing classes or curriculums. Whatever the disillusionment, remember that God is present in your life and will hold you in the palm of his hand. Everything, good or bad, has a reason. Even if you do not understand its purpose, be thankful to God for these moments or events. Ask God to turn your disappointments into hopefulness. God worked in Saint Patrick's life enabling him to escape slavery. After acquiring an education, Saint Patrick felt God called him to Ireland. There, he preached that the Trinity will sustain people despite misery. Reflect on your past disappointments and how you handled them. What can you do differently the next time with God's intervention? How can you be more trusting of God?

Dear God,

I place my fears, concerns, and hopes in your hands. Take my disappointments and transform them into something meaningful, but teach me patience while I wait for you. Amen.

Tuesday

> "I sought the LORD, and he answered me,
> delivered me from all my fears" (Psalm 34:5).

Talk to God today. Who isn't worried about final exams? If you are plagued with stress and uncertainty, seek God's guidance for direction. He wants to hear from you; so tell him what is in your heart. Set aside time to talk to the Lord because in doing so, God will advise you. Can you find a quiet place to have a conversation with the Lord? If there are distractions and interruptions you might miss his message. Saint Rafqa Petronilla al-Rayès sought divine guidance. This Lebanese woman was compelled to lead a religious life. Through her questioning, she heard God's voice sanctioning her desire when she looked at an icon of Our Lady of Deliverance. When you talk to God, can you look at a photograph of Jesus? Perhaps you can find a picture online. It may help to foster a divine connection between you and the Lord.

Dear God,

Help me to open my heart to you so I can tell you what I feel. Calm me so that I can speak to you and hear your message for me. Amen.

Wednesday

"Let us know, let us strive to know the LORD; as certain as the dawn is his coming. He will come to us like the rain, like spring rain that waters the earth" (Hosea 6:3).

Make friends with God. How would you become better acquainted with classmates? You could text them, have lunch with them, walk to class, or attend a lecture series. Surround yourself with friends because they will get you through rough patches at school. What are your rough patches? It is also important to get to know God. You can do that through prayer and revealing what you honestly feel in your heart. When you accept that Jesus died to forgive your sins and to give you eternal life in heaven, and live in accordance to God's law, our Lord will hear your cries and comfort you in your time of need. You can count on that as certainly as you expect the sun to rise and fall each day. What can you do today to take your relationship with God to the next level?

Dear God,

Help me to get to know you better. I want you to be my best friend forever. Amen.

Thursday

"Those who spare their words are truly knowledgeable, and those who are discreet are intelligent. Even fools, keeping silent, are considered wise; if they keep their lips closed, intelligent" (Proverbs 17:27–28).

Listen and be still. God gave you a beautiful mind and the ability to reason. Instead of trying to fix someone's problems, can you be there to listen or give them a shoulder to cry on? Often, that is all they need. They might work out their own troubles by having you there simply as a sounding board. Listening is a vital skill that will serve you well throughout your entire life. It will also help you to hear God's messages. Ask God to bless you with his wisdom during trying times. Is there someone in your life who needs you to listen to them? How can you develop your listening skills?

Dear God,

Help me to be a good friend to (_____). Whenever I listen to his problems, I want to jump in with solutions. Remind me to let him decide what is best. I ask this through your name, Lord. Amen.

Friday/Saturday

"The righteous holds to his way, the one
with clean hands increases in strength" (Job 17:9).

Living the righteous life is not easy. When the going gets tough, kick it up a notch. You chose your curriculum and college for a reason, and now it is your opportunity to make your dreams come true. God led you to this place and allowed doors to open for you. Your schoolwork is imperative. When God calls you to do something of great importance, do not let anything thwart your progress. Thank God for the obstacles in your path for it is a sign that you are headed in the right direction. As you prepare for final exams, what can you do to make your study time more productive? Could you pray before you head to the library or meditate during study breaks? What works best for you?

Dear God,

It is so confusing trying to decipher if I am doing the right thing when everything comes to me as a struggle. Bless my work, Lord, and help me to do well on my final exams. You are the reason for my existence. Amen.

Set Sail

Sunday

"But evils surround me until they cannot be counted.
My sins overtake me, so that I can no longer see.
They are more numerous than the hairs of my head;
my courage fails me. LORD, graciously rescue me!
Come quickly to help me, LORD!" (Psalm 40:13–14).

The Lord will help you. During finals week, it is understandable to feel edgy and overwhelmed with everything on your plate: exams, projects, papers. It's not only happening to you. Do not let issues escalate as life appears to unravel. Trust in God, asking him to be compassionate and fill you with his love. Give your worries to God. What can you do today to surround yourself with all that is good, loving, and beautiful? Is there a tranquil place on campus where you can be still and talk to God? While that might help you today, how can you align yourself more closely with the Lord throughout this week?

Dear God,

Calm me and fill me with your love so that I don't freak out with test anxieties. Keep me focused on you and everything that I learned this semester so that I will do well. Amen.

Monday

"He said: 'O LORD, my rock, my fortress, my deliverer,
my God, my rock of refuge! My shield, my saving horn,
my stronghold, my refuge, my savior, from violence you
keep me safe' " (2 Samuel 22:2–3).

The life of a student can be challenging. God has given you an important job as a college student at this juncture in your life. You are on the brink of completing an academic year that was full of hard work and brilliant accomplishments. Reflect on God's involvement in them. Another endurance test is required of you as you take final exams. Put your faith in God for enlightenment to recall the information that you have been studying. Ask God to be your refuge during this tumultuous time. As another semester draws to a close, put all of your faith in God. Ask him to keep you resilient as your summer plans unfold.

Dear God,

Help me to be the best that I can be. Give me the courage and wisdom to make sound decisions to reflect my past and spring toward my future. Everything that I do is in your name, Lord Jesus. Amen.

Tuesday

"With all vigilance guard your heart,
for in it are the sources of life" (Proverbs 4:23).

Make God your safety net. Marines are stationed throughout the world to ensure the safety of our country. Firewalls on your computer protect your information against viruses. Guardrails line highways to keep drivers safe on the roads. God has given you a safeguard to keep you on course as you journey through life: your heart, stirred by your passions and emotions. Guard your heart to stay focused on the path that God has chosen for you. Your heart is like your command center, guiding you through life. Protect your heart to keep evil from permeating, contaminating, and poisoning this very lifeline that you depend on. Believe that the Lord has your back. He will walk with you as you complete your projects and take exams. How will you protect your heart this summer?

Dear God,

Keep me on the straight and narrow path of righteousness so that everything I say and do is pleasing to you. Enable me to do well on tests and projects so that I can put my knowledge to good use. I ask this in your sweet and holy name. Amen.

Wednesday

"God is our refuge and our strength, an ever-present help in distress. Thus we do not fear, though earth be shaken and mountains quake to the depths of the sea" (Psalm 46:2–3).

God will keep you safe. Final exams and projects may seem like earthquakes in your life right now, but do not panic. If you should feel stress or worry, pray to God to clear your head so that you can think clearly. Ask God to fill you with courage. When you feel as if you are in a room with no doors or windows, God will point you in the direction of the exit. There is always a way out of every situation. Pray while you wait. God will come to your rescue. Close your eyes and imagine Jesus standing beside you, his arms around you, guiding you to a place of serenity. God will always be with you, no matter where you go and no matter what you do.

Dear God,

Take my stress and carry my burdens today. Allow me to do well on my exams and projects so that I can do your work and please you every day of my life. Amen.

Thursday

"Do not let love and fidelity forsake you; bind them around your neck; write them on the tablet of your heart. Then will you win favor and esteem before God and human beings" (Proverbs 3:3–4).

Have a loyal and faithful heart. It is so important to have a good reputation because it affects the way people think about you. The impression of professors, friends, and employers affects you. A good name commands respect. What do you do at school to uphold a good reputation? Contemplate ways you can set a shining example for others to emulate. How have your college experiences enhanced your character? God will grant you a good reputation when you are loyal to him and are kind and generous to everyone you meet. How have you grown individually over the academic year that will impact your family life once you settle back at home? How will you maintain a loyal heart as you transition home for the summer?

Dear God,

Allow virtuous thoughts to fill my head and heart. Work through me to keep my reputation solid and honorable throughout my college experience and my entire life. Amen.

Friday/Saturday

"May the God of endurance and encouragement grant you to think in harmony with one another, in keeping with Christ Jesus" (Romans 15:5).

Follow Jesus' example. What is your mantra? Make it be: what would Jesus do? Ask God to bless you with patience while you leave school and transition into a new endeavor this summer. Whether you attend summer classes, work at an internship in another city, or move back home with family, trust in God's plan for you. Learn from your successes and failures this past academic year. Turn to God, who will provide encouragement and endurance as you venture into your next stage of life. Develop tolerance for the idiosyncrasies of your neighbors and work toward a peaceful environment. God can give you the patience and fortitude you need to live harmoniously. You have studied, prayed, and put your best foot forward. Take the next step. Walk courageously with the Lord on your summer journey.

Dear God,

Fill me with patience and inspiration while I live through your magnificent example. Thank you, Lord, for your steady stream of gifts last semester. Keep me strong while I begin the next chapter of my life. Amen.

Summer Holidays:

3rd Sunday in May to Early August

These summer themes can be read according to need and desire.

If one theme does not apply to you this summer, simply move to ones that are more applicable to your life situation at the moment.

The themes selected here are based on some common events that take place for college students during summer holidays.

Just remember to pray, rejuvenate, and thank God as you enjoy these summer months—a well-deserved respite.

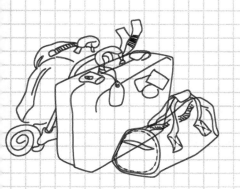

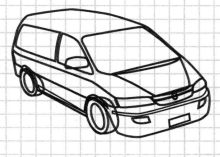

Internships

Have you ever wondered what your education was worth? Do you study your coursework and wonder how it will come together and apply to the "real" world? An internship opens a small window into your preferred profession. An internship can be a critical component of your education because it helps you to decide if you will enjoy working in your chosen occupation.

If this summer you are taking part in an internship, think about the person who first mentioned this opportunity to you. God brought that person into your life to present this prospect to you. It wasn't a happenstance occurrence but a part of God's plan. Consider your decision to seize an opportunity that will enable you to more fully comprehend the scope of your abilities to perform in this field of interest. You could love the internship, thus reaffirming that you have chosen the right career path, and will be eager to finish your program and obtain your degree. The possibility exists that you might dislike the job, which grants you time to find a new path by changing directions and explore something new. Either way, God has put this opportunity in your hands and only you can decide what to do with it. Just as in prayer, we must discern God's will for our lives, internships and life experiences teach us to discern our next steps. Use this opportunity to grow in your area of interest, and if the experience does not jibe with you, it is not too late to make a change.

Dear God,

Thank you for providing this wonderful opportunity to use my time and talents this summer at (_____). You must have enormous confidence in me. Please help me accomplish the task of front of me with dedication and precision. Amen.

Work

Will you spend a portion of your summer working? Have you applied for several jobs, wondering which one will be the best? The job you get might not be exactly what you had hoped for. Can you accept it with an open mind? If you need the money, working is a logical solution. Cash will come in handy next semester when you have bookstore bills or are in need of an occasional treat. Working is a fact of life; and it helps us to build our character.

Some summer jobs are enjoyable. Will this be your first job as a college student? Can you see God's hand guiding you toward one position? Perhaps there are special people God wants you to meet through this route of employment. Maybe the work itself will force you to rethink or confirm your career goals. This employment opportunity could open new doors to prospects that you never dreamed possible. Or maybe you are simply going back to a summer job you did in high school.

God loves you and believes in you. There is a genuine purpose for your summer job. How will you spend the remainder of the summer when you are not working? Perhaps your summer work will allow you the much-deserved and needed leisure such as quality time with friends and family, volunteering, or reading spiritual books for personal gratification. Put your trust in the Lord, who knows what is best for you.

Dear God,

Bless my decision to work this summer. Help me to be successful and to find many intrinsic rewards along the way. Make me a productive worker, touching the hearts of everyone I meet. Bring new people into my life and bless those relationships. I love you. Amen.

Vacation/Travel

Have you been blessed with the opportunity to take a vacation this summer? Will you take a "stay-cation" or travel to some exciting destination? Perhaps there are relatives you could reconnect with. Maybe you will meet new people in a strawberry patch or at a county fair. Your time away could be jam-packed with activities; exploring new places, trying different cuisines, or immersing yourself in diverse cultures.

Traveling is an educational experience in itself because there are so many steps involved in planning a trip, and no classes to teach you what to do. Often, you learn as you go serendipitously. Will you stay in the U.S. or travel overseas? How will you get there? What will you do and where will you stay? Is it safe? Who will travel with you? Is the trip affordable? How much stuff will you pack and how long will you be away? What is the purpose of this trip and what do you hope to get out of it?

Along your summer journey you could feel God's hand leading, guiding, and safeguarding you. While traveling is fun, it's nerve-racking, too. Remember that God goes everywhere with you, and if you find yourself in a quandary, call out to God for help. If you are concerned about directions, translations, safety, or other unsettling matters, ask God to bring someone to help you.

Dear God,

Show yourself to me in the people I meet through my summer travels. Bless my vacation and the experience that ensues so I can learn from them and grow as an individual as I expand my horizons. Keep me safe as I journey onward through life. You are my rock and salvation. Amen.

Reconnecting With Family and Friends

Does God want you to spend quality time reconnecting with your family? You are returning home as a new person, full of hopes and dreams, and full of wisdom from all of your college experiences. Are you satisfied with your personal growth? Your parents recognize you as their "child" who has grown and matured, and they are proud of your accomplishments. Cherish the time together, even if it is only for a few days—because quality time with your beloved friends and family members is a gift.

The ability to rejoin family functions, albeit temporarily, is healthy for you and them. From your parents you could seek wisdom about different opportunities you could try next semester. Perhaps you want to try a new living arrangement or switch curriculums. Parents and grandparents feel loved and useful when you solicit their advice. God brought you into your family for a reason. For most of us it is the place where we first feel cherished.

You might even be considering religious life as a priest or nun. Reflect and contemplate the type of service you wish to generate in your life.

Has God given you a chance to catch up with old friends from high school or church groups? Perhaps God wants you to build bridges and strengthen healthy relationships from your past that could be a source of camaraderie throughout your life.

Dear God,

Bless the relationships of those I love. Strengthen my bond and keep my love alive. Thank you for putting such wonderful people in my life. They formed me into the person I am today. I want them to be proud of me, so help me, Lord, to stay on the straight and narrow path when I am away from them. Keep them safe and well. I ask this in your holy name. Amen.

Relaxation

Your body is a temple. The Holy Spirit dwells within you (1 Corinthians 3:16). Therefore, take proper care of it by giving your body rest. This past academic year has been a marathon of sorts. You raced to the library, then back to your dorm to change books. You darted into the dining hall, grabbed a quick bite to eat, and scurried out the door to catch the next lecture. After a race like that, your body craves rest. The summer is the perfect time to recharge your batteries. How will you relax this summer?

Students mysteriously survive with severe sleep deprivation. The summer is the perfect time to catch up on your slumber. Summer is a great time to refuel and nourish your body with nutritious food, such as healthy vegetables, fruits, and nuts. Perhaps you could visit a farmer's market and meet the people who grow the food you eat. Learn about sustainable agriculture or food science over the summer to determine if either is an interesting field to study or work in some day. Could you volunteer in a food pantry in your community?

Your body also needs exercise. Maybe you could learn a new sport over the next few months. Just because you are not in school doesn't mean you can't learn something new. Take this opportunity as a sign from God to keep learning. Think differently now, and it could help you later.

Dear God,

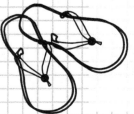

Bless my rest. Heal my body and make me whole again so I can return to school in August refreshed and invigorated to learn more. Thank you for summer sun and the chance to reconnect and relax with my family and friends around me. I adore you. Amen.

Summer Classes

Can you take extra classes through a community college, online, or through your university over the summer? It will lighten your load next semester and keep you focused throughout the summer by continuing to work in the "study mode." You could devote yourself to taking on one difficult class that necessitates extra attention and full concentration. Perhaps the summer classes will expose you to a new subject or field that you didn't previously consider. Maybe you could satisfy your "elective" class requirement over the summer and get it out of the way, making room in your schedule next semester for something bigger and better.

Taking classes is a great way to keep your mental state sharp. Instead of watching mindless television programs, can you be productive, fine-tuning your study habits so that in August you will be on the ball ready to jump-start the semester full throttle? Can you sign up for next semester's classes now, order your books online, and start reading them in advance? You are in the driver's seat of your education. Are you taking full advantage of every learning opportunity that comes your way? God will bless you for expending that extra effort. It takes perseverance and a high degree of motivation to continue studying throughout the summer.

Enjoy walking across a new campus and delight in the new friendships you will form with different classmates and professors. Only God knows why you were all brought together to study the same topic. Trust in the Lord that your summer will indeed be fruitful.

Dear God,

Bless me as I continue learning on another college campus. Open my mind to absorb the new course material. Make my summer an educational wonderland and help me to set aside time for fun and prayerful reflection. Amen.

Volunteering

Has God touched your heart in an unusual way to draw you to the needs of others? Have you heard God calling you? How will you answer? When you do God's work, he will help you overcome obstacles and transport you through any difficulty to see a project to fruition. When you do charitable work, God works through you.

In whatever venue you volunteer, whether it is with sick children, the elderly, or the impoverished, God will bless you for it. It is immensely rewarding to use your time and talents to give to others, even if you think you don't have any special skills to offer. If you search deep down inside, you will realize that you do have many distinctive abilities that you can share. When you give to others, you will feel special, loved, and needed. Whatever you put into this venture, you will get twice as much out of it!

Perhaps you could teach someone to speak English or provide instruction to someone who cannot read. Maybe you can assist in a vacation Bible school program at a nearby church. What lessons will you learn from volunteering? When you work with the less fortunate, you are, in a sense, touching God, because God is in each of us. When you look into the eyes of the destitute, you will see God.

Dear God,

Bless my ability to give to others. Make my heart malleable to encompass the love that I give so that it will resonate back to me. Enable me to do good deeds every single day this summer so that when I return to school, I will want to continue doing kind acts. Fill me with kindness, Lord. I trust you and love you. Amen.

Mission Trip

There are many ways you could give of yourself over the summer. Have you considered taking a mission trip? Whether you travel overseas to an impoverished nation or visit indigent families in America, it will please God. There are many needy people in the world. You don't have to look very far; there are disadvantaged people wherever you go, even in your own community.

God has equipped you with special talents that you can share. Smiling and offering kindness to those you meet is a gift, especially when you witness extreme poverty and dire situations among the weak, sick, and innocent. Putting someone at ease with a warm caress and gentle words removes the possibility of haughtiness and sets the tone for equality. Letting someone know you care is enough. You don't have to build a school or dig a well. Just being there and humbling yourself, and being willing to help in any way you can, is sufficient.

Pray and celebrate the glory of God with them. You have an amazing chance to meet and relate to people you would otherwise never know. God can bring you together and will allow you to be a part of the "big picture," making a difference. Imagine how wonderful it will be to return to school in the fall with gifts like that from the Lord!

Dear God,

Bless my decision whether or not to take a mission trip or work with impoverished people within my own community. Keep me safe and well so that I can do your work wherever I go. Keep me strong so that my actions make a difference to those I meet. I ask this in your holy name. Amen.

Study Abroad

Have you considered immersing yourself in a foreign culture, absorbing their rituals and traditions by traveling overseas? Have you been blessed with an opportunity to expand your horizons by embracing another way of life? Can you broaden your realm of possibilities by trusting in the Lord that this might be what he wants of you? It does not matter where you are in the world; God sees you and has directed you to that place for a special reason. You may not understand what that reason is; you merely need to trust in God who has a purpose for everything that happens. If you travel overseas, what are some ways you can be true to yourself by not compromising your own values and still do God's work?

You have the chance to decipher what ideas and traditions are favorable among other cultures that you want to incorporate into your own life. What imprint will you leave behind? Will it reflect your religious beliefs and ability to do God's work while you study abroad? What personal, academic, and spiritual goals do you hope to accomplish if you are overseas? Ask God for enlightenment to enable you to achieve your ambitions.

Dear God,

Bless my thoughts, hopes, and dreams of international travel and help me to make a difference by studying abroad. Soften my heart to love the people you put in my path. Keep my mind open to accept the differences I encounter while I learn and grow. Thank you for granting me this opportunity. Keep me safe and strong as I journey onward. Thank you, Lord, for your unconditional love. Amen.

Social Networking

The summer is an excellent time to step outside of your comfort zone to network with people who have the potential to help you. This could be an encouraging mentor who might coach you through the remainder of your college experience. Perhaps you could seek out your university alumni who reside nearby. Maybe there is a church member who is employed in the field you wish to enter. Is there a neighbor who can offer you pearls of wisdom? God puts special people in your path to help you.

The best way to seek out these individuals is to encounter people you normally might not speak to. Ask God for the courage and insight to approach and converse with them. They could offer you a chance to job shadow or volunteer in their place of employment. They may well arrange an abbreviated internship, which would enable you to determine if you are compatible for that type of work. Trust God to put the right people in your path to necessitate this. Networking is a way of life and is noted in the Bible. "Many curry favor with a noble; everybody is a friend of a gift giver" (Proverbs 19:6).

Dialog with friends about your future plans and desires. They might know someone who could be a good resource for you. The key is to expose your desires to people you may not know very well. It is difficult to open up yourself to vulnerabilities, but your willingness to be social and network could reap you many benefits in the long run.

Dear God,

Fill me with the knowledge and wisdom necessary to step forward and speak to those who can help my future dreams come true. Amen.

Fostering New Relationships

Throughout your college journey, God has brought many people into your life for a reason. You are reminded to turn to friends in time of need: "Do not give up your own friend and your father's friend; do not resort to the house of your kindred when trouble strikes. Better a neighbor near than kin far away" (Proverbs 27:10). Thus, it is wise to foster the friendships you have made throughout the college journey.

Camaraderie is enjoyable and entertaining. God wants you to celebrate, nurture, and cherish the companionships he has given to you. You might need each other some day to help one another through difficulties. Keep in touch with your friends over the summer while you are not busy with classes, and do not take them for granted. In order to keep friendships flourishing, you need to cultivate them. Can you communicate and relax with each other so that next semester your bonds of friendship will have strengthened? Friends are gifts from God, and friendships are gifts that we give to each other.

During your summer break, how can you make the effort to strengthen and develop new friendships? You can never have too many friends! God gave you everything you need to make a friend: an endearing smile, loving eyes, a warm heart, and a tender touch. The rest is up to you.

Dear God,

Thank you for blessing me with the ability to make and keep friends. Surround me with good people in my life so that I can lean on them during difficult moments. Make me strong so that they can lean on me when their need arises. Keep my bonds resilient, and let me be a reliable, trustworthy friend to everyone I know. I love you, Lord. Amen.

Making Future Plans

Before you plan ahead, reflect back to evaluate where you have been and what you have done. Were there any pitfalls you should avoid next semester? Did you do something that didn't go well and you want to change that behavior? How were your study habits? Did you socialize too much or not enough? Were you involved in enough clubs and activities or too many? What did you do that turned out exceptionally well that you want to repeat in the fall? What new adventures would you like to try next semester? What are your future goals?

"Watch carefully then how you live, not as foolish persons but as wise, making the most of the opportunity" (Ephesians 5:15–16). God places many opportunities in your path to ensure you a successful college experience. It is up to you to take advantage of them. Don't let dishonest people derail you. Stay focused. Only you can decide your future by the choices and plans you make. Pray on every decision. Ask God for enlightenment and to guide you as you go. When you get discouraged and don't know what to do, call out to God, then listen for his voice.

Pray every day. Eat healthy, well-balanced meals. Get exercise daily. Try to get at least seven hours of sleep each night. Study every day, even if you think you understand the material perfectly. Thank God for all he has given you, for all good gifts come from God.

Dear God,

Bless every decision I make. Make me an honorable student, wise beyond my years. Enable me to be a helpful classmate and a loyal friend to everyone I meet at school. Help me to be successful so that I do your work brilliantly. Amen.

About the Author

Barbara Canale's writing
career began in 1994 with the
publication of a nonfiction
book titled *Our Labor of Love:
A Romanian Adoption Chronicle*,
about her experiences adopting
two orphans with enormous
medical needs. Feeling God
calling her to change her life
drastically, she decided to write

about the sagas of raising post-institutionalized children
with unique medical problems. She documented her
daughters' growth and development through lighthearted
stories that she published in a variety of magazines, including
Seek, Exceptional Family, and *Whispers From Heaven*.

After many years of tending to her daughters'
medical needs and treatment that contributed to drastic
improvements, Barbara returned to her career as a healthcare
worker and wrote more spiritual pieces. She published
narrative inspirational stories for the *Chicken Soup for the
Soul* series.

In 2007, she began writing "The Word of the Lord," a
column for the Syracuse diocese's *Catholic Sun*. In addition,
she contributes journalistic pieces and inspirational stories
to fit the *Catholic Sun*'s needs. Also in 2007, she began
writing for *55 Plus Magazine*, a retirement publication, and
In Good Health—Central New York's Healthcare Newspaper.
Today, Barbara Canale is a full-time writer.